Wrap & Roll

Wrap & Roll

California Culinary Academy

Macmillan·USA

MACMILLAN
A Simon & Schuster Macmillan Company
1633 Broadway
New York, NY 10019-6785

Macmillan Publishing books may be purchased for business or sales promotional use.
For information please write: Special Markets Department, Macmillan Publishing USA,
1633 Broadway, New York, NY 10019-6785.

Production Coordinator and Editor: Paula J. Hamilton

Library of Congress Cataloging-in-Publication Data

Wrap & Roll / California Culinary Academy
        p.   cm.
    Includes index
    ISBN 0-02-862287-1 (alk. paper)
    1. Stuffed foods (cookery) I. California Culinary Academy.
    TX836.W73 1998
    641.8–dc21   97-38974
                                                        CIP

ISBN 0-02-862287-1

Book design by Amy Trombat

Manufactured in the United States of America
10 9 8 7 6 5 4 3 2 1

Acknowledgments

We thank the following faculty members and friends of the Academy for sharing their special wraps recipes and chef's tips: Mark Berlin, Linda Carucci, Winnie Chang, Mark Davis, Kevin Duffy, Shelley Handler, Kathleen Kennedy, Herve LeBiavant, Loretta Rampone, Peter Reinhart, Clyde Serda, Kristen Sikes, Sukhi Singh, Greg Tompkins, Jeanne Van Steen, and Rhoda Yee.

We also thank the following chefs for testing the recipes and for all of their helpful suggestions: Barbara Haimes, Martha Kroncke, Katy Ross, Arminda Schreil, and Thy Tran.

In addition, we thank Chef Jeff Hurst whose photographs were an invaluable help to Alan Witschonke who illustrated the various wrapping techniques.

And a special thank you is given to Chef Keith Keogh, president of the California Culinary Academy, for introducing a wide-ranging curriculum based on global cuisine and encouraging a whole generation of chefs to look beyond their borders for culinary inspiration.

Contents

Introduction

The classic tune "He's Got the Whole World in His Hands" has new meaning in culinary circles. Hand-held wrapped foods are all the rage. Almost every culture has created a "wrapped" dish whose popularity stretches far beyond the country's natural borders. Vietnamese spring rolls, Mexican tacos, Italian calzoni, English pasties, Indian samosas, and stuffed Greek grape leaves are only a few examples.

At the prestigious California Culinary Academy in San Francisco, international wraps are a favorite menu item. In an innovative curriculum that emphasizes global cuisine, students master the art of using Japanese sashimi knives and Chinese cleavers as well as classic French knives, as they deftly prepare Japanese sushi, Central American tamales, and French dessert crêpes each week for the Academy's restaurants and popular grand buffets.

Innovative chef-instructors teach students that the whole category of wraps offers a delicious opportunity to depart from tradition and explore fusion cooking at its finest. Chinese wontons, for example, are delicious stuffed with Western ingredients, including chiles, cheese, and fresh corn. Spring roll wrappers become a convenient jacket for crisp banana and chocolate fritters. And it took creative Academy chefs to put the corned beef inside, rather than beside, the cabbage and to fill Mexican flour tortillas with spicy Thai chicken, fragrant jasmine rice, and peanut sauce.

Most wraps and fillings are interchangeable. A savory smoked trout, caramelized onion, and potato filling is as delicious baked in buttery filo triangles as it is in a traditional empanada. Spicy red chile chicken works as successfully as a corn tamale filling as it does as a filling for steamed banana leaves. Roasted ratatouille takes as well to being baked in calzoni as it does in pesto-flavored crêpes.

Besides testing cooks' imaginations and pushing culinary boundaries, wraps serve several other important functions. Edible wrappers make dishes portable and easy to handle, and they are an excellent way to utilize leftovers. Next time you have some extra broiled salmon, remember the recipe for seafood ravioli filling. Give leftover mashed potatoes and roast chicken new life by turning them into stuffed potato pancakes. Blend grilled steak with warm apples and blue cheese and roll it in nutty-flavored buckwheat crêpes. Bake nearly any leftover in crisp golden leaves of filo and it will get an elegant second life.

This collection of favorite recipes from the chefs of the San Francisco–based California Culinary Academy includes classic as well as contemporary recipes for nearly every wrapped food from dolmas to dim sum. From the Academy's "Foods of the Americas" course come ideas for creating tamales and wraps using handmade corn and flour tortillas. Learn from our Asian chefs the secrets of using wonton and spring roll wrappers, as well as nori and dried bean curd sheets. Pastry and baking experts share their tips for making crêpes, stuffed breads, empanada pastry, and pie dough and for using filo. And from our garde manger kitchen there are ideas for turning vegetables—including cabbage, lettuce leaves, corn husks, banana leaves, and even mustard greens—into delicious hand-held appetizers and entrées. As wrappers, vegetables preserve flavor and keep in moisture, and in the case of corn husks, banana and grape leaves, and cabbage, they encourage low-fat cooking.

There are two rules to remember as you prepare to enjoy wrapped foods: (1) Most fillings, especially those for quick-cooking Asian wraps, stuffed pastas, and filo, must be cut into very small pieces to ensure even cooking. (2) Season fillings well. They must have bold enough flavors to stand up to their wrappers.

Wrapped packages have always promised surprise and delight. Wrapped foods are no different—they just happen to be low-fat, convenient, and tasty as well.

Cantonese Spring Rolls
Crispy Smoked Salmon Spring Rolls
Curried Chicken Purses
Mostly Vegetable Filipino "Lumpia"
Fresh Lumpia Wrappers
Truffled Banana Fritters
Fresh Vietnamese Spring Rolls with Shrimp
Crispy Vietnamese Spring Rolls
Siu Mai (Steamed Pork Dumplings)
Scallops with Chinese Vegetables in Crispy Pockets
Southwestern Wontons
Peek-a-Boo Shrimp Dumplings
Sichuan Preserved Mustard Greens with
Smoked Ham in Bean Curd Sheets
Vegetarian Maki Sushi
Teriyaki Tuna Hand Rolls
Char Shiu Bao (Steamed Pork Buns)
Char Shiu Marinade
Basic Bao Dough
Sweet and Sour Dipping Sauce
Orange Ponzu Dipping Sauce
Nuoc Cham (Spicy Fish Sauce)
Mango Chutney
Fresh Mango Salsa
Sweet Raisin Chutney
Tangy Apricot Sauce
Lumpia Brown Sauce
Kiwi Coulis
Tangerine Sauce

Asian Wrappers

Bite-size bundles of food wrapped in paper-thin noodles are a trademark of Chinese cooking. These little dumplings have been served with tea as far back as the Sung Dynasty in the tenth century. Loosely translated as "heart's delight," *dim sum* refers to the tradition of choosing one's favorite dumplings from an endless array that passes one's table. A leisurely morning spent selecting one dim sum after another, a national pastime in China, is becoming increasingly popular here in the United States.

Today most American supermarkets stock a wide range of prepared Asian wraps, allowing you to make spring rolls, wontons, pot stickers, and even Japanese sushi at home. These convenient wraps are also fantastic for making homemade ravioli or even wrapping around chocolate-stuffed bananas for an elegant contemporary dessert fritter.

Whether you're craving traditional favorites or exploring exciting new combinations, here is a food lover's guide to what may seem like a bewildering selection of Asian wraps.

Spring Roll Wrappers

Spring roll wrappers are very thin crêpes made from a dough of high-gluten flour and water. Cooked on a hot griddle, then pressed together and cut into 8-inch squares, these pale white wrappers are available in the frozen section of Asian and specialty markets. They are used throughout Southeast Asia, both fried and uncooked, for such favorites as Cantonese spring rolls and Filipino lumpias. While the name and filling may vary from country to country, the basic wrapping technique is the same for all.

Spring rolls are a traditional Chinese New Year's treat. Fried to a beautiful golden hue and stacked up high to resemble little gold bars, they symbolize prosperity in the coming year. The Chinese New Year, based on the lunar calendar, marks the beginning of spring; hence the name spring rolls. However, when spring rolls first appeared in the United States, eggs were one of the most popular fillings, and so these popular fried treats became known as "egg rolls."

Thaw an unopened frozen package of spring roll wrappers slowly in the refrigerator before using. With a sharp knife, trim off 1/4 inch from all the edges for easier separation of the wrappers. Store any unused wrappers, tightly wrapped in several layers of plastic wrap, in the refrigerator for up to two weeks or in the freezer for up to one month.

Spring rolls can be frozen before they are fried. Arrange them on a baking sheet seam side down, with at least 1/4 inch of space between the rolls, and place in the freezer until they are completely frozen, about 2 hours. The rolls can then be transferred to a freezer-safe plastic bag and frozen for up to one month. Do not thaw the rolls before frying; simply allow 1 to 2 minutes more cooking time. To reheat after cooking, arrange them in a single layer on a baking sheet and place in a 350°F oven until crisp and warmed through.

Tip: One of the most important rules to remember when making spring rolls is to make sure that the rolls are tight and that there are no air pockets or open corners. Use a mixture of flour and water to seal the wrapper. Make sure the filling is well chilled and very dry, adding cornstarch, if necessary, to thicken any excess liquid.

Vegetable Cutting Techniques

1a) Slicing thinly on a diagonal: Peel a carrot or other vegetable. Holding a cleaver or chef's knife at an angle (the smaller the angle, the longer the slices will be), cut through the carrot into thin slices.

2a) Cutting a scallion julienne: Trim the root end and any wilted leaves from the scallion.

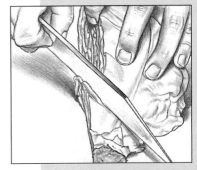

3a) Removing the core of a cabbage: Cut the head of cabbage through the core into quarters. Place each section flat on a cutting board. With a sharp knife, make a 45-degree-angle cut into the cabbage above the exposed core and cut away the core.

b) Cutting thin julienne: Stack the thin slices of carrots in a pile, with each slice stacked slightly to the left of the one preceding it. Cut through the stack, using the slices as straight edges, forming thin julienne.

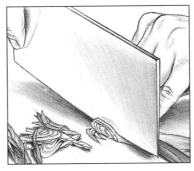

b) Taking advantage of the scallion's natural structure, thinly slice it diagonally.

b) Shredding cabbage: Once the cabbage has been cut into quarters and the core removed, cut straight down through the cabbage to make thin shreds.

Cantonese Spring Rolls

This traditional appetizer is served throughout China, but the vegetables in the filling and the accompanying sweet-sour sauce reveal the Cantonese roots of the rolls.

If you can't find fresh water chestnuts, substitute fresh jicama; canned water chestnuts lack the distinctive sweetness and crunch that are essential to the filling. Chef Rhoda Yee likes to cut these crispy golden rolls in half and arrange them cut side up on serving plates, with a small dish of dipping sauce on the side.

1 teaspoon cornstarch

1 teaspoon soy sauce

1 teaspoon rice wine or dry sherry

6 ounces lean pork, finely julienned (about 1 cup)

2 tablespoons canola, peanut, or corn oil for stir-frying

2 cups finely shredded Napa cabbage

1 cup mung bean sprouts

1/2 cup finely julienned bamboo shoots

1 stalk celery, finely julienned (about 1/2 cup)

1/2 cup finely julienned fresh water chestnuts or jicama

6 dried shiitake mushrooms, soaked in hot water for 30 minutes, drained, and finely julienned

3 scallions, sliced diagonally into 1-inch lengths

1 teaspoon salt

1/2 teaspoon sugar

2 tablespoons cornstarch dissolved in 1/4 cup chicken stock

2 tablespoons oyster sauce

1/4 cup all-purpose flour

1/4 cup cold water

1 package (1 pound) spring roll wrappers, edges trimmed 1/4 inch

Canola, peanut, or corn oil for deep-frying, about 6 cups

Prepare the filling: In a medium bowl, combine the 1 teaspoon cornstarch, the soy sauce, and rice wine. Add the pork, stir to coat evenly, and marinate in the refrigerator for 15 minutes.

Wrapping Cantonese Spring Rolls

Trim off any dried edges of the wrappers to make them easier to separate

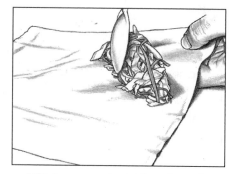

With the wrapper turned like a diamond shape and the smooth-side-down, one corner facing you, place about 1/4 cup of the filling in a straight line about 3 inches long and 1 inch above the corner closest to you

Heat 1 tablespoon of the oil in a wok or large frying pan. Add the Napa cabbage, bean sprouts, bamboo shoots, celery, water chestnuts, and mushrooms. Stir-fry for 3 to 4 minutes, or until the vegetables have begun to wilt. Transfer the vegetables to a large bowl and set aside.

Heat the remaining 1 tablespoon of oil in the pan. Add the marinated pork and stir-fry for 2 to 3 minutes, until the meat is no longer pink. Return the vegetables to the pan and add the scallions, salt, sugar, cornstarch-stock mixture, and oyster sauce, stirring to combine well. Cook for 1 to 2 minutes, or until the liquid is absorbed. Correct the seasoning, adding more salt, if necessary. Transfer the filling to a shallow bowl or baking sheet and set aside to cool.

To wrap the spring rolls: In a small bowl, mix together the flour and cold water until completely blended. Have ready the filling, the trimmed wrappers, and a tray or large plate for the rolls. For step-by-step wrapping and cooking techniques, see instructions and illustrations below and on page 8.

To serve: With a serrated knife, cut each spring roll in half diagonally. Arrange them on serving platters accompanied by Sweet and Sour Dipping Sauce (page 43), Tangerine Sauce (page 47), or Fresh Mango Salsa (page 45).

Fold the wrapper over the filling and tuck the end tightly underneath the filling.

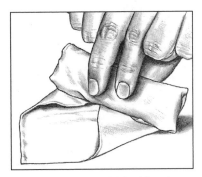

Fold in the left and right sides of the wrappers, angling them in slightly so that the finished roll will have tight corners. Then continue rolling the wrapper up snugly, stopping about 2 inches from the opposite corner.

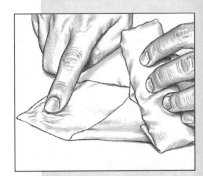

Dab a small amount of the flour paste on the open corner of the wrapper and continue rolling up the spring roll. Press the end to seal.

Frying Cantonese Spring Rolls

Heat about 3 inches of oil in a wok or heavy saucepan to about 360°F (drop a small piece of the wrapper into the oil; it will immediately bubble and start to brown). Slowly lower the spring rolls into the hot oil to prevent splashing. Avoid overcrowding, which will lower the temperature of the oil.

Fry the spring rolls about 3 minutes on each side. Use tongs, long chopsticks, a wire mesh spatula, or a slotted spoon to turn the rolls over so that they brown evenly.

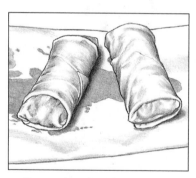

Remove the rolls and let drain on a tray lined with paper towels.

Crispy Smoked Salmon Spring Rolls

1 tablespoon olive oil

2 heads of baby bok choy, cut into very thin strips (about 1 cup loosely packed)

1 small carrot, julienned

2 cloves garlic, minced

1 package (1 1/2 ounces) mung bean thread noodles, soaked in hot water for 10 minutes, drained, and cut into 2-inch lengths

1/3 cup dried tomatoes, soaked in hot water for 30 minutes, drained, and finely diced

1/2 cup fresh basil leaves, cut into very thin strips

1 teaspoon salt

1/2 teaspoon freshly ground white pepper

1/4 cup all-purpose flour

1/4 cup cold water

8 spring roll wrappers, edges trimmed 1/4 inch

1/4 pound smoked salmon, sliced 1/8 inch thick across the grain into 3-inch-long strips

Canola, peanut, or corn oil for deep-frying

Makes 8 spring rolls

A favorite appetizer in the Academy's Tavern, Chef Kathleen Kennedy's crisp spring rolls combine Asian techniques with popular California flavors. If you can't find baby bok choy, substitute Napa cabbage or spinach. You can also use lightly sautéed shrimp in place of the smoked salmon. Provide small dishes of Orange Ponzu Sauce (page 43).

Prepare the filling: Heat the olive oil in medium frying pan over high heat. Sauté the bok choy about 1 minute, or until barely wilted. Add the carrot and garlic; cook 1 minute more. Transfer the vegetables to a large bowl and stir in the mung bean thread noodles, dried tomatoes, and basil. Season with the salt and pepper.

To wrap the spring rolls: In a small bowl, mix together the flour and cold water until completely blended. Have ready the vegetable and noodle mixture, the trimmed wrappers, and the salmon strips. For step-by-step wrapping and cooking techniques, see the instructions and illustrations on pages 8–10, placing a slice of smoked salmon on top of the filling before wrapping each roll.

To serve: Cut each spring roll in half diagonally. Arrange cut side up on a serving platter and accompany with a small bowl of Orange Ponzu Dipping Sauce (page 43), Fresh Mango Salsa (page 45), or Nuoc Cham (page 44).

Curried Chicken Purses

Makes 20 purses

Eastern ingredients and flavors are combined with Western techniques to produce appetizers that look like attractive little bundles tied with green ribbons.

2 bunches scallions

1 large russet potato, peeled and cut into $1/2$-inch cubes

1 tablespoon oil

1 small yellow onion, minced

$1/2$ pound ground chicken

2 large cloves garlic, finely chopped

$1^1/2$ teaspoons curry powder

$1/2$ teaspoon ground cumin

Juice of $1/2$ lemon (about $2^1/2$ tablespoons)

2 tablespoons chopped fresh cilantro

$1/2$ teaspoon salt

1 package (1 pound) spring roll wrappers, edges trimmed $1/4$ inch

Canola, peanut, or corn oil for deep-frying

Prepare the filling: Bring a medium saucepan of salted water to a boil. Trim the green tops from the scallions, setting aside the white bulbs. Blanch the green tops in the boiling water just until they are wilted, about 15 seconds. With a slotted spoon, immediately transfer the green tops to a large bowl of iced water to stop the cooking, then spread them out on paper towels to dry. Mince the reserved white bulbs.

Add the diced potato to the boiling water and cook until tender, about 5 minutes. While the potato is cooking, heat the 1 tablespoon of oil in a large frying pan over medium heat. Add the minced onions and cook until they soften, about 1 minute. Add the chicken and cook, stirring occasionally, until it is no longer pink, about 5 minutes. Then add the garlic, curry powder, and cumin; cook for another 2 minutes to bring out the flavor of the spices. Transfer to a large bowl. When the potato is done, drain and lightly mash it, then stir into the chicken mixture along with the lemon juice, cilantro, and salt. Set the filling aside to cool.

To prepare the purses: Working with 4 wrappers at a time, place about 1 tablespoon of the filling in the middle of each. Lift up and gather the sides of the wrapper, forming a pouch that completely encloses the filling. Secure each purse by carefully tying the folds together just above the filling with one of the green onion tops. Gently fan out the corners of the wrapper.

In a wok or heavy, deep saucepan, heat about 3 inches of oil to about 350°F. (The oil is hot enough when a strip of the spring roll wrapper bubbles immediately when dipped into it.) Fry the purses, 4 or 5 at a time, turning once, until each is golden brown on all sides, about 3 minutes per batch. Remove with a slotted spoon and drain on paper towels. Transfer to a serving platter and serve with Sweet Raisin Chutney (page 45) or Tangy Apricot Sauce (page 46).

Mostly Vegetable Filipino "Lumpia"

2 tablespoons canola oil

6 scallions, minced

1/4 pound coarsely chopped chicken, turkey, pork, or beef

1/4 pound green beans, trimmed and thinly sliced diagonally

1 small sweet potato, peeled and cut into 1/4-inch cubes

1 small russet potato, peeled and cut into 1/4-inch cubes

8 large shrimp, peeled, deveined and minced, (about 1/2 cup)

3 cloves garlic, minced

1/2 small head cabbage, finely shredded (about 1 1/2 cups)

1 cup cooked chickpeas

1 medium carrot, cut into 1/4-inch cubes

1 cup chicken stock

2 tablespoons finely chopped fresh cilantro

2 teaspoons salt

1 tablespoon sugar

1/2 tablespoon freshly ground black pepper

1 tablespoon cornstarch dissolved in 2 tablespoons cold chicken stock

2 heads of green leaf or red leaf lettuce

24 Fresh Lumpia Wrappers (recipe follows)

1 cup shelled peanuts, chopped

Lumpia Brown Sauce (page 46)

Makes 24 lumpias

Traditionally, lumpia is made with a flour-based wrapper, then deep-fried and served wrapped in a lettuce leaf with a garlic-vinegar dipping sauce. In this fresh version, a piquant brown sauce, chopped peanuts, and an egg-battered wrapper add a contemporary twist.

Prepare the filling: Heat the oil in a wok or large frying pan over medium-high heat. Add the scallions and stir-fry until softened, about 1 minute. Add the chicken and cook until the meat is no longer pink, about another 2 minutes. Add the green beans and potatoes and cook for 2 to 3 minutes. Add the shrimp and garlic and continue cooking and stirring for another 2 minutes, or until the shrimp turn pink.

Stir in the cabbage, chickpeas, carrot, stock, cilantro, salt, sugar, and pepper; cook until the vegetables are tender but still crisp, 3 to 4 minutes. Add the dissolved cornstarch and cook for 1 minute more, or until the sauce thickens. Transfer the filling to a large bowl and set aside to cool.

Separate lettuce into individual leaves; rinse well, pat dry, and remove any thick stems. Arrange the lettuce leaves, wrappers, filling, peanuts, and brown sauce on a serving tray and let each person wrap his or her own lumpias.

To wrap lumpia rolls: Lay a lettuce leaf on a clean, dry surface with the stem end closest to the edge of the counter. Place a wrapper on top of the lettuce, allowing the frilly top of the lettuce to extend beyond the wrapper's top edge. Place about 1/4 cup of the filling on the wrapper and sprinkle about 1 teaspoon of peanuts over the filling. Bring the right and left sides of the lettuce over the filling, overlapping them slightly in the center. Roll up the end of the lettuce closest to you, leaving the top open. Repeat with the remaining filling and wrappers. Serve immediately with the brown sauce.

Fresh Lumpia Wrappers

Makes about 24 lumpia wrappers

Cornstarch adds a delicate texture to these crêpe-like wrappers. They can be made several days ahead, wrapped well in plastic and stored in the refrigerator.

1 cup cornstarch or rice flour
1/8 teaspoon salt
1 1/2 cups water

3 eggs
2 tablespoons canola oil
2 tablespoons butter, melted

In a large bowl, combine the cornstarch and salt. Add the water and beat until smooth. Beat in the eggs and oil until well combined. Cover and refrigerate the batter for at least an hour.

Heat a small, preferably nonstick frying pan over medium-high heat. Brush it lightly with the melted butter. Spoon about 1/4 cup of batter into the center of the pan, then quickly tilt and swirl the pan until a thin layer of batter covers the bottom of the pan. Cook until the bottom of the wrapper is lightly browned, about 45 seconds. Turn the wrapper out onto wax paper and let it cool. Repeat with the remaining batter, placing a sheet of wax paper in between each wrapper to prevent them from sticking to each other. If not using the wrappers immediately, wrap them tightly in plastic and refrigerate.

Truffled Banana Fritters

2 tablespoons heavy cream

1 1/2 ounces hazelnut gianduia, coarsely
    chopped, or 3 tablespoons Nutella

1 ounce bittersweet chocolate,
    coarsely chopped

3 large, ripe bananas

3 ounces finely diced, toasted hazelnuts,
    about 3/4 cup

6 spring roll wrappers

1 egg, lightly beaten

Corn or canola oil for deep-frying

Confectioners' sugar

Makes 6 fritters

Gianduia, a rich and silky chocolate flavored with hazelnuts, is available in specialty food shops, but Nutella makes a fine substitute.

Tip To skin and toast whole raw hazelnuts, heat the nuts in a 350°F oven for 10 to 15 minutes to dry out the skins. Then place a handful at a time in a clean, dry kitchen towel. Fold the towel over the nuts and rub vigorously to loosen the skins. Discard the loosened skins. You can toast the nuts on a baking sheet in a 325°F oven for 5 to 7 minutes, or until golden brown and very fragrant. The nuts can also be toasted in a large frying pan over medium heat. They scorch easily, so be sure to keep an eye on them to prevent burning.

Prepare the hazelnut ganache: In a small saucepan, bring the cream to a boil. Remove the pan from the heat and stir in the gianduia and bittersweet chocolate until the mixture is melted and smooth. Set aside to cool and thicken slightly.

Prepare the filling: Peel and cut each banana in half crosswise. Then split each piece in half lengthwise. Pipe a layer of hazelnut ganache down the center of a banana piece. Sprinkle with toasted hazelnuts and top with a matching banana piece to form a sandwich. Repeat until all of the banana pieces have been filled.

To wrap the fritters: Place each stuffed banana about an inch from the bottom edge of a spring roll wrapper. Roll the wrapper over the banana. Bring the right side of the wrapper over the filling, forming a neat and snug right angle. Fold the left side of the wrapper over the filling, forming a neat and snug right angle. Brush the beaten egg on the top edge of the wrapper. Complete the spring roll by rolling it snugly shut. Let it sit for a few minutes to make sure the edge is sealed. If not, repeat the process. Wrap the remaining stuffed bananas in the remaining spring rolls.

To cook: In a wok or large, heavy frying pan, heat 1 1/2 to 2 inches of oil to about 350°F. (It's hot enough when the end of the spring roll bubbles immediately when dipped into the oil.) Fry 3 to 4 spring rolls at a time, being careful not to crowd them, until they are golden brown on all sides, about 3 minutes. Remove and drain them on paper towels.

To serve: Cut each fritter in half diagonally, dust with confectioners' sugar, and arrange on serving plates. Drizzle with Kiwi Coulis (page 46) and Tangerine Sauce (page 47).

Rice Paper Wrappers

These unusual wrappers from Vietnam are formed from a batter of rice flour and water. Traditionally, the mixture was poured in thin rounds onto woven bamboo mats and left to dry in the sun to a brittle, translucent white sheet. Now rice paper is produced in large factories, but the classic imprint of the woven mats is still recreated on these distinctive wrappers.

Rice paper is used uncooked as a wrapper for both hot and cold fillings, and may also be deep-fried as a wrapper for spring rolls. The most commonly used shape is the 8-inch round. In order to use the wrappers, simply soak them a few at a time in warm water for about 30 seconds, then arrange them in a single layer on a clean kitchen towel. Let set 2 or 3 minutes, until soft and pliable. For deep-frying the wrapper, dissolve about 1 tablespoon sugar in the soaking water; the sugar will caramelize and give the spring rolls a golden brown color. The rice paper, once rehydrated, will stick to itself quite readily. Arrange the filled rolls with the seam side down to help seal the rolls before serving or frying.

The dried rice paper can be stored easily in a cool, dry place for an indefinite time. Because the rounds break easily, make sure they are stored on a flat surface. It is best to eat both fresh and fried rolls as soon as possible. However, the fresh rolls can be individually wrapped in plastic wrap and stored for a few hours in the refrigerator, and the fried rolls can be reheated on a baking sheet in a 350°F oven until warmed through and crisp.

Tip: When deep-frying these rolls, make sure the oil is on a relatively low heat, about 325°F. This will allow the inner layers of the rice paper to cook to a crisp texture without the outer layers getting too brown.

Fresh Vietnamese Spring Rolls with Shrimp

4 ounces rice sticks

1 medium carrot, finely shredded

2 teaspoons fish sauce

18 medium shrimp (about $^{1}/_{2}$ pound), cooked, peeled, and chilled

12 sprigs cilantro

2 inches of English cucumber, cut in half lengthwise, then thinly sliced into 24 half-circles

36 fresh mint leaves

$^{1}/_{4}$ cup roasted peanuts, roughly chopped

3 scallions, green part only, finely minced

12 (8-inch) round rice paper wrappers

$^{1}/_{2}$ cup Nuoc Cham (page 44)

Makes 12 spring rolls

These translucent rolls are as beautiful to look at as they are delicious. This is a favorite creation of Chef Linda Carucci. For parties she likes to arrange all of the filling ingredients in the center of the table and encourage her guests to create their own rolls.

Prepare the filling: Place the rice sticks in a large bowl. Cover with boiling water and let stand until the noodles have softened, about 5 minutes. Strain the noodles through a fine-mesh sieve and rinse with cold water until they are cool. Drain the noodles well and roughly chop them. Set aside in a small bowl.

In another small bowl, toss the shredded carrot with the fish sauce. Slice each shrimp in half lengthwise. Set up an assembly line of small bowls of ingredients in the following order: cilantro, cucumber, mint, noodles, peanuts, seasoned carrot, scallions, and shrimp.

To soak wrappers: Follow the instructions on page 16.

To wrap: Follow the instructions and illustrations on page 18.

To serve: Cut each roll in half diagonally. Set the halves on end with the cut side up and drizzle about 1 teaspoon of Nuoc Cham (page 44) on each half.

Have ready the ingredients for the filling, including softened rice sticks, shredded carrots and scallions, sliced cucumbers, cooked shrimp, and mint leaves.

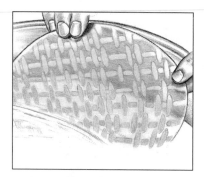

Soak each rice paper round in warm water for about 30 seconds, until it is soft and pliable.

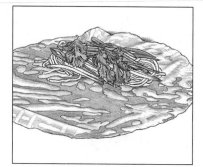

Lay the softened rice paper on a clean surface with the smooth side down. Arrange the filling ingredients in a 4-inch line about 3 inches from the edge of the wrapper closest to you.

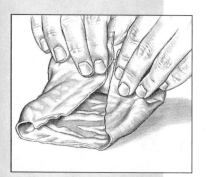

Lift the edge of the wrapper over the filling and roll one full turn, tucking the rice paper tightly around the filling. Fold both the left and right sides of the wrapper over the filling, angling the sides slightly toward the center.

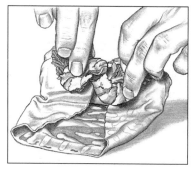

Arrange 2 shrimp halves and 2 mint leaves on top of the roll. Then continue rolling up the wrapper tightly.

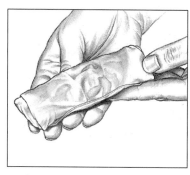

Press the end of the rice paper lightly to adhere it to itself. The shrimp and mint leaves will be visible through the rice paper.

Crispy Vietnamese Spring Rolls

1 package (1 1/2 ounces) mung bean thread
    noodles, soaked in hot water for
    10 minutes and drained

4 dried shiitake mushrooms, soaked in hot
    water for 30 minutes and drained

1 tablespoon cornstarch

2 tablespoons cold water

1 tablespoon canola, corn, or vegetable oil

4 ounces ground pork (about 1/2 cup)

1/2-inch piece of ginger, peeled and minced
    (about 1 tablespoon)

2 cloves garlic, minced

1 cup finely chopped Napa cabbage,
    loosely packed

1 cup roughly chopped mung bean sprouts

1 medium carrot, grated

1/2 cup finely chopped fresh water chestnuts
    (about 8) or jicama

2 scallions, finely chopped

3 tablespoons chopped fresh mint

3 tablespoons chopped fresh cilantro

2 tablespoons fish sauce

1 teaspoon salt

1/2 teaspoon sugar

1/4 teaspoon ground white pepper

2 tablespoons sugar dissolved in 2 cups
    warm water

1 package (12 ounces) 8-inch round rice
    paper

Canola, peanut, or corn oil for deep-frying

Makes 24 spring rolls

Traditionally, crispy hot spring rolls are wrapped in lettuce leaves with cucumbers and fresh herbs, then dipped in spicy Nuoc Cham sauce (page 44). This version adds extra zing to the rolls by incorporating the herbs into the filling as well.

Prepare the filling: Cut the mung bean thread noodles with scissors into 1-inch lengths and set aside. Trim and discard the woody stems from the shiitake mushrooms and mince the caps; set aside. In a small bowl, dissolve the cornstarch in the cold water.

Heat the 1 tablespoon of oil in a wok or skillet over high heat. Add the pork, ginger, and garlic and stir-fry until the meat is no longer pink, about 2 minutes. Add the cabbage, bean sprouts, carrot, water chestnuts, and reserved mushrooms; stir-fry 2 to 3 minutes longer, or just until the vegetables are wilted. Be careful not to overcook them. Add the scallions, mint, cilantro, fish sauce, salt, sugar, white pepper, and reserved cornstarch mixture. Toss in the noodles, mix well, and transfer the mixture to a large bowl; let cool completely.

To wrap the spring rolls: In a shallow bowl, mix together the sugar and warm water until completely blended. Soak the wrappers a few at a time in the sugar water for about 30 seconds, then arrange them in a single layer on a clean kitchen towel. Have ready the cooked and cooled filling and the rice paper wrappers rehydrated with sugar water. Follow the wrapping instructions and illustrations on page 20.

To cook: Heat 4 inches of oil in a wok or large, deep, heavy frying pan to about 325°F. Deep-fry the spring rolls, a few at a time to prevent them from sticking to each other, until golden brown on all sides, about 5 minutes.

Serve the spring rolls hot with green leafy lettuce, fresh mint leaves, cilantro sprigs, and sliced serrano chiles and accompany with Nuoc Cham (page 44).

Wrapping Crispy Vietnamese Spring Rolls

Place about ¹/₄ cup of the cooked filling in a straight line about 3 inches long and 1 inch from the edge of the softened rice paper closest to you.

Fold the wrapper over the filling and tuck the end tightly underneath the filling. Then fold in the right and left sides of the wrappers, angling them in slightly so that the finished roll will have tight corners. Continue rolling up the wrapper tightly around the filling. See the figures on page 10 on how to deep-fry them.

To serve, wrap the deep-fried spring roll in a crisp lettuce leaf with mint, cilantro, and sliced chile peppers.

Siu Mai Wrappers

Made with high-gluten flour, water, eggs, and salt, these ultra-thin, slightly translucent wrappers are used for a very popular dim sum dumpling dish. Only $3^{1}/2$ inches in diameter, the rounds come in 14- to 16-ounce packages found in the refrigerated sections of Asian markets, large supermarkets, and specialty food shops.

Because the wrappers are so thin, the color of the filling shines through slightly after steaming, creating an interesting effect. It's important not to expose too many wrappers at once to air so that they won't dry out.

Siu mai wrappers can be stored in the freezer, tightly wrapped in multiple layers of plastic freezer wrap, for up to one month. Make sure to thaw them overnight in the refrigerator. Once the dumplings are formed, arrange them $1/2$ inch apart on a baking sheet lightly dusted with flour and place in the freezer for about 2 hours, until frozen. Then pack them in recloseable plastic freezer bags and store them in the freezer for up to a month. Frozen siu mai do not need to be thawed before cooking, simply cook them the same way as if they are fresh, adding an extra 2 minutes or so to the cooking time.

General Steaming Tips

1) When steaming, use high heat, but make sure the dumplings are located well above the water source so the rolling boil of the water does not come in contact with the delicate dumplings.

2) A traditional bamboo or metal steamer unit can be purchased, but isn't necessary. Steamers can easily be created using what is available in most kitchens. For example, place a flat strainer lined with cheesecloth over a pot of the same size. Create a makeshift cover with heavy-duty aluminum foil.

Siu Mai (Steamed Pork Dumplings)

Makes about 48 dumplings

$^1/_2$ *pound shrimp, peeled, deveined, and*
    coarsely chopped

1 pound ground pork

4 dried shiitake mushrooms, soaked in
    warm water for 1 hour, drained,
    and minced

1 tablespoon cornstarch

2 teaspoons sugar

$^1/_2$*-inch piece of ginger, minced*

2 cloves garlic, minced

$^1/_4$ *teaspoon salt*

$^1/_8$ *teaspoon five-spice powder*

1 tablespoon Chinese soy sauce, preferably
    dark or mushroom flavored

1 tablespoon oyster sauce

2 teaspoons rice wine or dry sherry

1 teaspoon sesame oil

6 fresh water chestnuts, peeled and minced
    (about $^1/_3$ cup)

1 package (14 ounces) siu mai wrappers

Prepare the filling: In a mixing bowl, combine the shrimp, pork, mushrooms, cornstarch, sugar, ginger, garlic, salt, and five-spice powder. Add the soy sauce, oyster sauce, rice wine, sesame oil, and water chestnuts and mix well.

To wrap: Gather together the filling and the wrappers. For wrapping instructions, see the illustrations on page 23.

To cook: See general steaming illustrations on page 23. These dumplings will take about 10 minutes.

To serve: Serve with a simple sauce of equal parts light soy sauce and white-wine or rice vinegar because the dumplings are already very flavorful.

Wrapping Siu Mai Dumplings

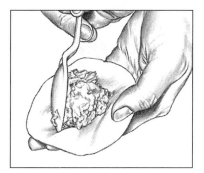

Hold the siu mai wrapper in your left hand and place a heaping teaspoon of filling in the center of the wrapper.

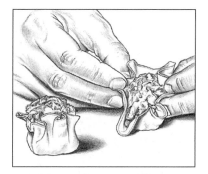

With your thumbs and the middle fingers of each hand, pinch the edge of the wrapper toward the filling at 6 equidistant points. Then press the pleats in firmly and gently squeeze the dumpling to adhere the wrapper to the filling and to create a waist-like indentation. The filling should be visible at the top through the gathered pleats.

For a decorative touch, wrap and tie a blanched scallion around the waist of the dumpling.

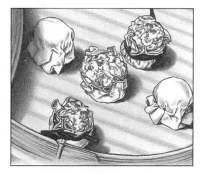

Line a steamer basket with parchment or wax paper. Arrange the dumplings at least $1/2$ inch apart with either the filling showing at the top or the open side down.

Wonton Wrappers

Made with high-gluten flour, water, eggs, and salt, these thin wrappers are cut into 3-inch squares and usually sold in 1-pound packages. Wonton wrappers are generally available in three different thicknesses.

As a rule of thumb, the thinner wrappers are for wontons to be cooked in water, and the thicker ones are for wontons to be deep-fried.

These wrappers can be stored in the freezer, tightly wrapped with multiple layers of plastic freezer wrap, for up to one month. Make sure to thaw them overnight in the refrigerator. Once the dumplings are formed, arrange them 1/2 inch apart on a baking sheet lightly dusted with flour and place in the freezer for about 2 hours, until frozen. Then pack them in recloseable plastic freezer bags and store them in the freezer for up to a month. Frozen wontons do not need to be thawed before cooking, simply cook them the same way as if they are fresh, adding an extra 2 minutes or so to the cooking time.

Scallops with Chinese Vegetables in Crispy Pockets

1 tablespoon cornstarch

1/4 cup chicken stock

2 tablespoons rice wine

2 teaspoons minced ginger

1 clove garlic, minced

1 teaspoon salt

1 teaspoon sugar

1/2 teaspoon sesame oil

1/2 pound bay scallops (about 1 cup)

3/4 cup fresh corn kernels or thawed
    frozen kernels

1/2 cup fresh or frozen green peas

1/2 cup chopped fresh water chestnuts
    (about 8) or jicama

1 small carrot, cut into 1/4-inch cubes
    (about 1/2 cup), blanched for 2 minutes

2 tablespoons minced Chinese chives

1 package (1 pound) wonton wrappers,
    medium thickness

1/2 cup water

Corn, peanut, or canola oil for deep-frying

Makes about 36 wontons

Serve these crispy appetizers with a dipping sauce made of equal parts light soy sauce and rice vinegar. Add a dash of hot chile oil if your palate craves a bolder flavor.

Prepare the filling: In a small saucepan, dissolve the cornstarch in the chicken stock. Stir in the rice wine, ginger, garlic, salt, sugar, and sesame oil. Bring the mixture to a simmer over medium heat, stirring constantly, until the sauce thickens, about 3 minutes. Remove the saucepan from the heat. Stir in the scallops, corn, peas, water chestnuts, carrot, and chives; set the mixture aside to cool.

To wrap: Have ready the filling, wrappers, and water. With the wrapper turned like a diamond, place a teaspoon of the filling in the center of the wrapper. Brush water on the edges of the top two adjacent sides. Fold the wrapper in half diagonally matching the bottom and top corners forming a triangle. Press the edges to seal. Repeat with the remaining ingredients.

To cook: Follow the frying procedure shown for spring rolls on page 10.

Serve immediately with dipping sauce made with equal parts of light soy sauce and rice vinegar.

Southwestern Wontons

Makes about 48 wontons

Combining a flavorful filling of corn, chiles, and cheese with convenient Chinese wonton wrappers creates an interesting bridge between East and West. For special occasions, add $1/2$ cup flaked crabmeat. Serve with fresh salsa.

1 cup shredded cheese (Monterey Jack, cheddar, mozzarella, or a combination)

$1/2$ cup fresh corn kernels or thawed frozen kernels

$1/2$ cup roasted and diced Anaheim or other mild green chiles, fresh or canned

3 scallions, thinly sliced

2 tablespoons chopped fresh cilantro

$1/2$ teaspoon salt, or to taste

1 package (1 pound) wonton wrappers, medium thickness

$1/2$ cup water

Corn, peanut, or canola oil for deep-frying

Prepare the filling: In a medium bowl, lightly toss together the cheese, corn, chiles, scallions, cilantro, and salt until thoroughly combined.

To wrap: Have ready the filling, wrappers, and water. Follow the instructions and illustrations on page 27.

To cook: Follow the deep-frying method illustrated on page 10.

To serve: Serve immediately with fresh salsa.

Wrapping Southwestern Wontons

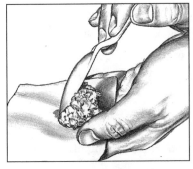

Holding the wonton wrapper in the palm of your left hand, place a heaping teaspoon of the filling about 1/2 inch up from the corner closest to you.

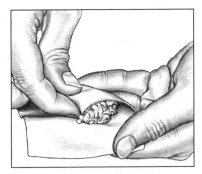

Fold the wrapper over the filling and tuck the end tightly underneath the filling. Then continue rolling tightly, stopping about 1 inch from the opposite corner.

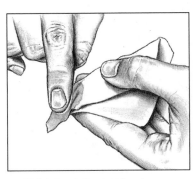

Lightly brush the right-hand corner of the wrapper with water.

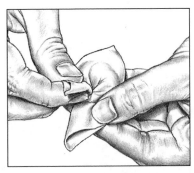

Place the left-hand corner of the wrapper on top of the moistened right-hand corner forming a hat, and press to seal.

Starch Dough

This particular recipe uses a mixture of tapioca starch and wheat starch moistened with boiling water. Tapioca starch lends a translucence to the steamed dumplings, allowing the colors of the filling to shine though. Traditionally, these dumplings are filled with shrimp to lend a beautiful pink color; however, vegetables can be used for their many bright shades as well.

Tip: When making the dough, be sure to stir vigorously while adding the boiling water so the entire dough is cooked all the way through, preventing the formation of small pearls in the dough. Depending on the humidity in the air, the dough may require more wheat starch.

Peek-a-Boo Shrimp Dumplings

SHRIMP FILLING

$1/2$ pound shrimp, peeled, deveined, and coarsely chopped

$1/2$ cup coarsely chopped fresh water chestnuts or jicama

1 scallion, finely minced

1 tablespoon rice wine or dry sherry

1 tablespoon egg white

1 teaspoon minced ginger

1 teaspoon cornstarch

$1/2$ teaspoon salt

$1/2$ teaspoon sesame oil

$1/4$ teaspoon sugar

STARCH DOUGH WRAPPER

1 cup packed wheat starch

$1/2$ cup tapioca starch

1 cup water

$1^1/2$ teaspoons canola oil

Makes 36 dumplings

Once steamed, the delicate starch dough of these dumplings becomes translucent, allowing the pretty pink color of the shrimp filling to "peek" through. There are two ways to form these dumplings, pleated in a half-moon shape or formed into a three-cornered hat. Illustrations of both methods are shown on pages 30–31.

The consistency of this dough is like Play-Doh™. If the first try is less than perfect, the dough can easily be reshaped. The simplest way to roll out the dough is to use a tortilla press; however, a flat metal spatula or cleaver will also work to flatten the balls of dough into rounds. Both wheat and tapioca starches are available at Asian markets.

Prepare the filling: In a large bowl, combine the shrimp, water chestnuts, scallion, rice wine, egg white, ginger, cornstarch, salt, sesame oil, and sugar; stir to combine thoroughly. Cover the bowl with plastic wrap and refrigerate.

Prepare the dough: In a medium bowl, stir together the wheat and tapioca starches. In a small saucepan, combine the water and oil and bring to a boil. Working quickly, pour the boiling water over the starches and stir vigorously until the mixture comes together into a soft dough. Remove the dough from the bowl and knead it until it is completely smooth. The dough should be moist but not sticky. If the dough feels too wet, dust lightly with additional wheat starch and continue to knead until the added starch has been incorporated. Tightly wrap the dough in plastic wrap until ready to use.

Divide the dough into 3 equal portions. Using your hands, roll each into a $1/2$-inch-diameter log. Cut each log into 12 pieces and roll each piece into a ball. Cover the balls of dough with a damp kitchen towel to keep them moist while you are rolling.

The easiest way to roll out the balls of dough is to flatten them with a tortilla press between 2 sheets of plastic film or wax paper. Each ball should form a round wrapper about 3 inches in diameter.

Tip See general steaming

tip in the Siu Mai section

(page 23).

To wrap: Follow the instructions and illustrations below and on page 31.

To cook: Place the dumplings close together, but not touching, on a lightly oiled pie plate. Place the plate inside a bamboo steamer over a wok or inside an aluminum steamer. Fill the wok or bottom of the aluminum steamer with 1 to 2 inches of boiling water. Cover the wok or steamer and steam the dumplings until the dough becomes translucent and the filling pink, about 7 minutes. Remove the dumplings from the steamer and cool them slightly before transferring them to a serving platter.

To serve: Serve the dumplings with a small dish of light soy sauce for dipping.

Making Triangle-Shaped Peek-a-Boo Shrimp Dumplings

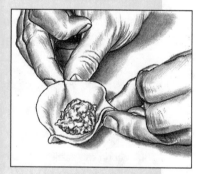
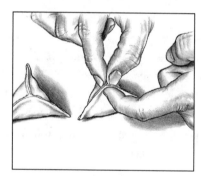
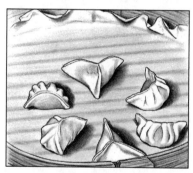

Place a heaping teaspoon of filling at the center of the flattened round of wheat starch wrapper. At 3 equidistant points around the edge of the wrapper, pinch firmly to make a triangular shape.

Starting from the pinched corners, lift the edges of the wrapper up over the filling and press together to seal. The dumpling will look like a three-cornered hat.

Line a steamer basket with parchment or wax paper and arrange the dumplings 1/2 inch apart.

Making Crescent-Shaped Peek-a-Boo Shrimp Dumplings

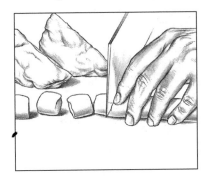

Divide the dough into 3 equal portions. Roll each portion into a 1/2-inch-thick log. Then cut each one into 12 equal pieces.

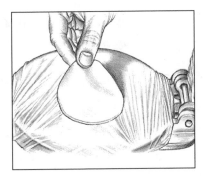

After rolling each piece of dough into a ball between the palms of your hands or against the work surface, flatten the ball into a thin round about 3 inches in diameter, using a tortilla press lined with plastic wrap.

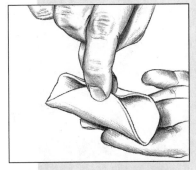

Place about a teaspoon of filling slightly off-center in a wrapper. Fold the wrapper in half over the filling, pinching it shut at the midpoint and leaving the sides open.

On the left side of the dumpling, make 3 tiny pleats each about 1/4 inch apart toward the center midpoint and press the pleated side to the bottom smooth side, sealing the filling in.

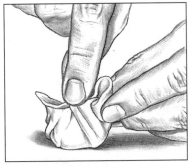

Repeat on the right side of the dumpling, forming the pleats toward the center.

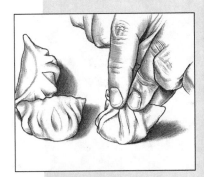

Place the wrapped dumpling on the counter and flatten the bottom slightly so it won't roll around.

Dried Tofu Skins

Made by heating soy milk until a coagulated "skin" forms on top, this yellow-hued wrapper is then laid out to dry. Extremely brittle and delicate, tofu skin needs to be rehydrated in warm water before use. The filled skin can be deep-fried for a delicately crispy texture or braised for a softly chewy texture. If it is to be deep-fried, a thick mixture of flour and water serves as a sealer; cornstarch is needed for dusting the skin before deep-frying to absorb excess moisture on it.

Sichuan Preserved Mustard Greens with Smoked Ham in Bean Curd Sheets

1 package (6 to 8 ounces) bean curd sheets

1 cup julienned smoked ham (about 5 ounces)

1 cup bean sprouts, blanched for 30 seconds and drained

1/2 cup julienned Sichuan pickled mustard greens, rinsed

1/2 cup canned whole baby ears of corn, sliced into 1/4-inch-thick rounds

1/2 cup julienned bamboo shoots

6 dried shiitake mushrooms, soaked in warm water for 1 hour, drained, and julienned

1-inch piece of ginger, finely julienned (about 2 tablespoons)

2 scallions, thinly sliced diagonally

2 tablespoons flour

2 tablespoons water

SAUCE

3 tablespoons cornstarch

3 cups chicken stock, preferably homemade or low-sodium canned

2 tablespoons soy sauce

1 tablespoon rice wine or dry sherry

1 teaspoon sesame oil

1/2-inch piece of ginger, minced (about 1 tablespoon)

3/4 teaspoon sugar

Pinch of freshly ground white pepper

5 sprigs cilantro, coarsely chopped

Makes 24 rolls, 2 rolls per serving

Prepare the wrappers: Soak the bean curd sheets in warm tap water for 20 minutes, or until pliable. Carefully remove them from the water and place between paper towels to remove the excess water. Cover with a moist kitchen towel to prevent them from drying out.

Prepare the filling: In a medium bowl, combine the ham, bean sprouts, mustard greens, corn, bamboo shoots, mushrooms, ginger, and scallions. Toss the ingredients until they are thoroughly mixed. In a small bowl, combine the flour and water; stir until completely blended.

To wrap: Cut each bean curd sheet into 6-inch squares. Place the point of one square facing you. Then place 1 rounded tablespoon of filling an inch above the lower corner of the bean curd sheet. Spread the filling out in an oval about 3 inches long. Fold the lower corner over the filling. Fold the right and left sides toward the center. Roll up the dumpling to the top corner and secure with a dab of the sealer. Place the rolls on a tray with the seam side down.

To cook: In a large saucepan, stir the cornstarch in the chicken stock until dissolved. Stir in the soy sauce, rice wine, sesame oil, minced ginger, sugar, and white pepper. Bring the mixture to a boil over medium heat, then reduce the heat to a simmer and cook, stirring, until the sauce thickens. Add the bean curd rolls to the sauce with the seam sides down. Cover the pan, and gently braise the rolls for 15 minutes.

To serve: Drizzle the rolls with the sauce and garnish with cilantro.

Nori

Dried nori seaweed is delicate in both texture and taste. It is packaged in several different forms and shapes. The most common is nori used for maki sushi, or rolled sushi. These sheets are toasted but not seasoned, and they are typically sold in a package of ten 7 x 8-inch sheets. Once opened, they should be kept in airtight bags and stored in a cool, dark place. A few passes over an open flame (gas burner) is enough to crisp the nori and turn it a slightly brighter green color. Other varieties of nori include a seasoned version that is typically used in shredded form as a garnish or simply eaten with steamed rice and plain nori.

The Japanese once wrapped raw fish in vinegared cooked rice as a way to preserve the fish when traveling or eating away from home. Originally only the fish was eaten, but as time passed, the rice that enclosed the fish became ritualized in its preparation, and the entire parcel was eaten. Nori was wrapped around the rolls for ease of handling and to keep the roll intact.

There are various types of maki sushi. All use nori as the wrapper, and their names vary based on shape, size, or filling. For example, if a roll is made into a cone shape, it is called te-maki sushi (or hand roll). If it's a thick roll filled with various components, it is called futo-maki. Kappa-maki are thin rolls with two ingredients, while rolls with only a single ingredient, such as cucumber, are known as kyuri-maki.

Cooking Sushi Rice

Sushi rice will be labeled medium grain in Japanese markets. Its shorter grains and slightly sticky consistency are essential in forming sushi rolls. Be sure not to confuse it with glutinous rice (also known as sweet rice), a dessert rice with very short, round grains that are extremely sticky.

The rice should be washed before using to remove any talc or glucose that the manufacturer may have used to help absorb excess moisture. Place the rice in a bowl, cover with at least 4 inches of water, then stir the rice and water in a few circular motions. Carefully pour off the water and repeat the process two more times. Once the rice is washed, try to drain off as much of the milky liquid as possible from the rice. Pour both the rice and the amount of water necessary to cook the rice into the container that you will be cooking the rice in. Allow the rice and water mixture to stand for 30 to 60 minutes so that the rice

Tip When rolling with nori, make sure the smooth, glossy side is facing out. Sealers are not necessary, since the moisture from the rice in the filling will permeate through and act as a sealer. The key is to place the seam side down for about 2 minutes before slicing to allow the nori to seal itself.

Dampen the knife with a wet cloth before slicing the sushi rolls so the blade will not stick to the rice. Make sushi to order; the rice will harden if refrigerated.

will expand; this ensures even cooking of the rice grains because the rice will absorb water more gradually.

There are several ways to cook sushi rice. Different amounts of water will be necessarily depending on the method, the thickness of the pot used, the amount of rice cooked, the heat source, and even the age of the rice. Experiment a few times to determine the ratio of water you need for your pot and for each new bag of rice you buy.

On the stovetop: You will need slightly more water using this method because of steam evaporation, about $1^1/4$ cups of water to 1 cup of rice. Place the water and washed rice in a heavy pot. While you don't want to use a pot that is too large, keep in mind that the rice will double in volume as it cooks. Bring the mixture to a boil over medium heat. Stir the rice once quickly to make sure no grains are sticking to the bottom of the pot, then cover the pot and reduce the heat to low. Allow the mixture to simmer and steam until the water has been absorbed, 12 to 15 minutes. Avoid lifting the lid too many times. The more rice you are making, the more time it will require. Remove the pot from the stovetop and allow the rice to rest, covered, for 10 to 15 minutes. Fluff the rice with a fork before using or serving.

In a steamer: Use about 1 cup of water to 1 cup of rice. Place the water and the washed rice in a container that will fit in the steamer with at least 1 inch of space to spare. Cover tightly with foil and steam for about 20 minutes. Remove the container from the steamer and set aside, unopened, to rest for 10 minutes. Remove the foil and fluff the rice.

In a rice cooker: Follow the manufacturer's guidelines. Typically the rice-to-water ratio is about 1 to 1. Always fluff rice before serving or using.

After the sushi rice is cooked, place it in a large bowl and fluff with a wooden rice paddle or large rubber spatula.

Pour the seasoned vinegar evenly over the rice. Coat each grain of the rice with the vinegar by gently lifting and turning over the rice in a folding motion, scraping the spatula along the bottom of the bowl. Be careful not to pack or break up the rice kernels.

Vegetarian Maki Sushi

3 cups uncooked sushi rice

4 small carrots, quartered lengthwise

16 dried shiitake mushrooms, soaked in hot
water for 30 minutes and drained

1/3 cup mirin

1/3 cup plus 2 tablespoons soy sauce

3/4 to 1 cup seasoned rice vinegar

1 English cucumber, peeled and cut into
strips 1/4 inch thick and 8 inches long

8 pickled daikon, cut into strips 1/4 inch
thick and 8 inches long

8 sheets nori

2 teaspoons wasabi powder, or more
to taste

Makes 8 sushi rolls, 64 pieces

This recipe shows how simple it is to take the classic technique for making sushi and then improvise to fit your own taste. Try using blanched asparagus spears, julienned strips of zucchini, avocado, sweet red and yellow peppers, or your favorite combinations of the vegetables listed in this recipe. You'll find mirin, sweet cooking sake, pickled daikon, wasabi—a fiery green horseradish—and bamboo rolling mats at Japanese groceries and large supermarkets.

Prepare the filling: Cook the rice following the washing and cooking instructions on page 34. While the rice is cooking, blanch the carrot strips in a small saucepan of boiling water for 3 minutes. Transfer to iced water to stop the cooking, then drain and set aside. Trim the woody stems from the mushrooms and discard; cut the mushrooms in half and set aside. Bring the mirin and 2 tablespoons of the soy sauce to a boil in a small saucepan. Add the sliced mushrooms and simmer, uncovered, until the liquid is completely absorbed, about 5 minutes. Set the mixture aside to cool.

Combine the cooked sushi rice with the seasoned vinegar according to the instructions and illustrations on page 36.

To wrap: Have ready the seasoned rice, blanched carrots, mushrooms, cucumber, pickled daikon, and nori. Follow the wrapping instructions on page 40.

With a sharp knife, cut each sushi roll in half, then cut each half in half again. Finally, cut each quarter in half. This method ensures that all the rolls will be evenly cut into 8 pieces.

In a small bowl, combine the wasabi and remaining 1/3 cup soy sauce; stir until completely blended. Serve the rolls immediately, accompanied by the wasabi dipping sauce.

Place a sheet of nori on top of a bamboo sushi mat. Moisten your hands with water. Pat a 1/4-inch-thick layer of sushi rice on the nori, leaving a 2-inch border at the top.

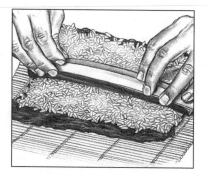

On top of the rice, arrange the filling ingredients in a straight line about 2 inches from the edge closest to you.

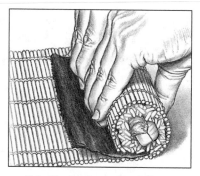

Using the bamboo mat to help you, lift the edge of the rice-covered nori and begin tightly rolling the nori and rice around the filling.

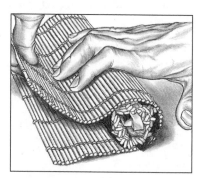

Continue rolling, lifting the excess bamboo mat up as you roll. Press the uncovered border of nori against the roll to seal.

Use a slightly dampened sharp knife to cut the sushi roll into 6 slices.

Teriyaki Tuna Hand Rolls

1 cup uncooked sushi rice
1/2 cup seasoned rice vinegar
1/2 cup mirin
1/3 cup plus 3 tablespoons soy sauce
4 teaspoons vegetable oil
1 pound fresh yellowtail or albacore tuna,
    sliced 1/2 inch thick
1/2 English cucumber, peeled and julienned

1 medium carrot, julienned
1 ounce of radish, daikon, or alfalfa sprouts,
    roots trimmed
1 bunch enoki mushrooms
6 sheets nori
2 teaspoons prepared wasabi

Makes 10 to 12 rolls

With the contemporary twist, this classic te-maki sushi is served with cooked and seasoned tuna. The best way to serve these rolls is to arrange all the filling ingredients in small bowls and have your guests roll their own. This way the nori will stay nice and crisp, and everyone can participate.

Prepare the sushi rice: Cook the rice following the washing and cooking instructions on page 34. Mix the rice with the vinegar following the instructions on page 36.

Prepare the teriyaki sauce: In a small saucepan, combine the mirin, 3 tablespoons of the soy sauce, and 2 teaspoons of the oil. Bring the mixture to a boil over medium heat, then reduce the heat to low and simmer the sauce until syrupy and reduced by half, about 5 minutes. Set the teriyaki sauce aside to cool.

Prepare the tuna: Heat a large frying pan over high heat until it is hot. Lightly coat the pan with the remaining 2 teaspoons oil and continue to heat until the oil is very hot but not smoking. Sear all the tuna pieces in the pan for about 1 minute on each side, until they are well browned and have very crisp crust. Transfer the seared fish to a platter and brush each piece with the teriyaki sauce; let stand for about 5 minutes to allow the tuna to cool slightly. With a sharp knife, cut the tuna into strips about 1/2 inch thick and 3 to 4 inches long.

To wrap: Have ready the sushi rice, tuna, cucumber, carrot, sprouts, mushrooms, and nori. Follow the wrapping instructions on page 38.

To serve: Place the wasabi and remaining 1/3 cup soy sauce in serving bowls and provide individual small dipping bowls. Each diner will mix his or her own dipping sauce according to taste.

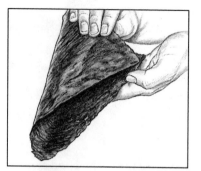

Fold a sheet of nori in half diagonally. Pinch the nori along the fold. It will break cleanly along the fold into 2 triangles.

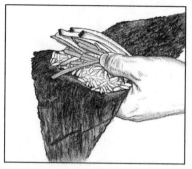

Holding a triangle of nori with the long side in your left hand, place 2 heaping tablespoons of sushi rice in a 1-inch-wide band about 1 inch above the center of the long side of the nori to about 1 inch from the opposite corner. Arrange strips of the filling on top of the rice, ending with a layer of the fish.

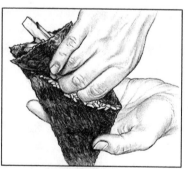

Lift the right-hand corner of the nori up and over, lining the edge of the nori next to the left edge of the rice, forming a cone shape.

Lift the left-hand corner of the nori up and over, completing the cone, and serve.

Char Shiu Bao
(Steamed Pork Buns)

2 pounds boneless pork shoulder or butt,
*   cut in long 1 1/2-inch-wide strips*
1 recipe Char Shiu Marinade
*   (recipe follows)*

2 tablespoons honey
1 recipe Basic Bao Dough (recipe follows)
Flour for dusting

Visitors to Chinatown can't help but notice huge steamer baskets filled with these smooth white buns. One bite and you'll know why they are a favorite dim sum treat.

In a bowl, toss the pork strips in the marinade and let the mixture stand in the refrigerator for at least 3 hours or overnight.

Preheat the oven to 400°F. Pour off the marinade from the pork and reserve it. Place the pork on a wire rack over a roasting pan with 1 inch of water and roast it for 15 minutes. (If you do not have a rack, you can place the pork directly on carrot or celery sticks arranged on the bottom of a roasting pan.) Turn the pork over and brush it with the reserved marinade. Reduce the heat to 375°F and continue roasting 25 minutes longer, basting occasionally with marinade, until the pork is well done.

While the pork finishes cooking, put the remaining marinade in a saucepan, bring it to a quick boil, and reduce to a glaze. Set the marinade aside to cool. Remove the pork from the oven, and brush it immediately with the honey. Let it cool, then cut it into 1/4-inch cubes. Toss the pork with the reserved marinade.

Place the dough on a lightly floured surface, flatten it slightly, and divide into 2 equal pieces. Roll each piece into a 12-inch-long log. With a sharp knife, slice each log into 1-inch pieces and place each piece on a floured surface. Cover the pieces with a slightly damp kitchen towel or plastic wrap to keep them from drying out while you are forming the baos one at a time.

Form each piece of dough into a ball, then flatten it slightly. With a rolling pin or dowel, roll each piece of dough from the edge to the center and back again, rotating the dough between turns, to form a 4-inch round that's slightly thicker in the center. Place the round of dough in your left hand, then place about 1 tablespoon of pork in the center. Using all 5 fingers of your right hand, grab the edges of the dough and gently pull the dough up, enclosing the filling. Twist the bao counterclockwise with your left hand as you twist clockwise with your right hand, pinching to seal the dough. Pinch off and discard any excess dough.

Place the buns, pinched side down, on 3-inch squares of parchment paper. Cover the buns with plastic wrap or a clean kitchen towel as you work. Let the buns rise for about 1 hour, or until doubled in size.

Pour about 1 inch of water into a wok or steamer. Arrange the buns about 1 inch apart on several steamer racks. Place the racks in the steamer, cover, and steam the buns over high heat for 10 to 12 minutes, until firm. Resist peeking while the buns are steaming or they might not rise. Serve within 4 hours or refrigerate and steam again before serving.

Char Shiu Marinade

A classic marinade for pork, this sauce is equally delicious with roast chicken and duck. It keeps well in the refrigerator for up to a week.

1/2 cup firmly packed brown sugar
3 tablespoons soy sauce
3 tablespoons hoisin sauce
2 tablespoons dry sherry

2 tablespoons yellow bean paste or yellow miso (optional)
1 teaspoon five-spice powder (available at large supermarkets and Asian markets)

In a bowl, combine all the ingredients and mix well. Refrigerate until ready to use.

Basic Bao Dough

Makes enough dough for 24 buns

Vary this basic dough by kneading in chopped garlic chives, lemon or tangerine zest, a pinch of star anise, crushed Sichuan peppercorns or some grated fresh ginger. After resting overnight, the dough is ready for stuffing and steaming.

1 1/2 teaspoons active dry yeast
2 tablespoons sugar
1 cup lukewarm water (110°F)

4 cups all-purpose flour, plus extra for dusting
3 tablespoons lard or shortening

In a bowl, stir the yeast and sugar into the warm water and let stand in a warm spot until the mixture is bubbly, about 10 minutes. Stir in 2 cups of the flour, blending well to form a thick batter. Then cover the starter and let it stand for about 1 hour, or until doubled in size.

In a large bowl, use a fork or pastry blender to cut the lard into the remaining 2 cups flour until crumbly. Stir in the yeast mixture to form a soft dough. Turn the dough onto a floured surface and knead it for 2 minutes.

Place the dough in a bowl. Cover the bowl with a damp towel or plastic wrap and let it rise for about 1 hour, or until doubled in size. Punch the dough down, wrap it well in plastic wrap, and refrigerate overnight.

Sauces

Serve the sweeter sauces, chutneys, fruit salsas, and sweet and sour dipping sauces with any of the fried items. The lighter soy sauce–based dipping sauces are best served with steamed dim sum. Nuoc Cham is a Vietnamese sauce that's typically served with both deep-fried and fresh spring rolls. Wasabi and soy sauce mixtures are preferred for sushi.

Sweet and Sour Dipping Sauce

Makes about 2 cups

2 tablespoons water

1 tablespoon cornstarch

3/4 cup rice vinegar

1/2 cup sugar

1/2 cup orange juice

1 tablespoon ketchup

1/2 teaspoon salt

In a small bowl, combine the water and cornstarch, blending well; set aside. In a small nonreactive saucepan, combine the rice vinegar, sugar, orange juice, ketchup, and salt; stir until smooth. Bring the mixture to a boil over medium heat, then reduce the heat to medium-low. Gradually stir the cornstarch mixture into the sauce, a little at a time, and simmer until the sauce thickens, about 2 minutes.

Orange Ponzu Dipping Sauce

Makes 1 cup

1/3 cup rice vinegar

1/3 cup orange juice

1/4 cup soy sauce

2 tablespoons sesame seeds

Combine all the ingredients in a blender. Process on high speed until smooth, about 3 minutes, scraping down the sides of the blender jar as needed.

Nuoc Cham (Spicy Fish Sauce)

Makes about 3/4 cup

1/4 cup lime juice
1/4 cup sugar
1/4 cup fish sauce

4 Thai chile peppers, minced with seeds
2 cloves garlic, minced
2 tablespoons water

In a small bowl, combine all the ingredients and stir until the sugar is completely dissolved. Let the sauce stand at least 30 minutes to allow the flavors to meld.

This sauce should be sweet, sour, and spicy. If you can't find fiery Thai chile peppers, substitute seeded and minced red jalapeños. If the flavor still isn't hot enough, add a pinch or two of cayenne pepper.

Mango Chutney

Makes about 6 cups

2 large ripe mangoes
1/4 ripe pineapple
3/4 cup firmly packed brown sugar
3/4 cup golden raisins
1/2 cup cider vinegar
1/2 cup dry white wine
1/4 cup diced red bell pepper

1/4 cup diced green bell pepper
1 small bay leaf
1/2 teaspoon salt
1/4 teaspoon cayenne pepper
1/8 teaspoon ground cloves
1/2 cup chopped walnuts

Stand a mango upright with the narrow side toward you. Make a vertical slice about 1/2 inch to the right of the stem so that it barely clears the long, flat seed. Repeat on the other side. Trim the flesh around the mango seed and cut it into small cubes. Score the flesh of each side into small cubes, cutting to but not through the skin. Press on the skin side of each half so that the cut side pops outward, hedgehog fashion. Slice the cubes of flesh from the mango skin and place them in a nonreactive saucepan. Repeat with the other mango.

Peel the pineapple, cut the fruit into small cubes, and place them in the saucepan. Stir in the sugar, raisins, vinegar, wine, peppers, bay leaf, salt, cayenne, and cloves. Bring the mixture to a boil. Boil for 5 minutes. Remove the saucepan from the heat. Stir in the walnuts and let cool. Store the chutney in the refrigerator for up to a month.

Fresh Mango Salsa

Makes 1 cup

1 large ripe mango
1/2 small red onion, finely chopped
1 tablespoon finely chopped fresh cilantro
1 tablespoon lime juice (about 1/2 lime)
1 green jalapeño chile, seeded and minced

1 clove garlic, minced
1/2-inch piece of ginger, minced (about 1/2 tablespoon)
1/4 teaspoon salt
Pinch of sugar

Stand the mango upright with the narrow side toward you. Make a vertical slice about 1/2 inch to the right of the stem so that it barely clears the long, flat seed. Repeat on the other side. Trim the flesh around the mango seed and cut it into small cubes. Score the flesh of each side into 1/4-inch cubes, cutting to but not through the skin. Press on the skin side of each half so that the cut side pops outward, hedgehog fashion. Slice the cubes of flesh from the mango skin and place them in a glass, ceramic, or other nonreactive bowl. Add the onion, cilantro, lime juice, jalapeño, garlic, ginger, salt, and sugar and gently toss to mix evenly. Cover and let stand in the refrigerator for at least 1 hour to allow the flavors to meld.

Sweet Raisin Chutney

Makes 1 cup

1/4 cup tamarind paste
1/2 cup water
1/4 cup packed light brown sugar
3 tablespoons golden raisins

1/2 teaspoon ground cumin
1/2 teaspoon ground ginger
Pinch of cayenne pepper
Pinch of salt

In a small bowl, mix the tamarind paste and water with a fork until well blended. Strain the mixture through a fine sieve into a blender, discarding the solids. Add the sugar, raisins, cumin, ginger, cayenne, and salt; puree to a thick, smooth sauce. If it appears watery, add more raisins and puree again. Let stand in the refrigerator for at least 4 hours before serving.

Tangy Apricot Sauce

Makes 1/2 cup

1/2 cup apricot preserves
2 tablespoons sugar
Grated zest and juice of 1 lemon

2 tablespoons orange juice
1/8 teaspoon salt

Combine all the ingredients in a small nonreactive pan and bring to a simmer over medium heat. Cook until thickened and smooth, about 2 minutes; transfer to a small serving bowl and let cool. Serve at room temperature.

Lumpia Brown Sauce

Makes 2 cups

1/2 cup firmly packed brown sugar
2 tablespoons cornstarch
2 teaspoons salt
2 cups water

Pinch of freshly ground white or
*   black pepper*
1/4 cup soy sauce
2 cloves garlic, minced (optional)

In a medium saucepan, combine all the ingredients and stir until completely blended. Bring the mixture to a boil over high heat, stirring constantly, and cook until the sauce thickens, about 2 minutes. Transfer the sauce to a serving bowl and let cool slightly before serving with fresh lumpia.

Kiwi Coulis

Makes about 1 cup

3 large ripe kiwis, peeled and coarsely chopped

Puree the kiwis in a blender or food processor. Press the puree through a fine strainer into a medium bowl; discard the seeds and pulp. Refrigerate until ready to serve.

Tangerine Sauce

Makes about 1 cup

2 teaspoons cornstarch

1 tablespoon cold water

1 cup tangerine juice

In a small bowl, dissolve the cornstarch in the cold water. In a small saucepan over medium heat, bring the tangerine juice to a simmer. Stir in the cornstarch mixture and continue simmering, stirring constantly, until the sauce is thick and translucent, about 2 minutes. Transfer to a serving bowl and let cool slightly.

Best Calzone Dough

Red Potato and Broccoli Stuffed Calzone

*Sautéed Chicken and Mediterranean
Vegetable Stuffed Calzone*

Roast Vegetable and Goat Cheese Calzone

Peppery Polenta Stromboli

Stuffed Yeast Breads

Yeast tops the culinary world's list of greatest discoveries. Historians generally agree that the momentous event occurred in Egypt around 6,000 years ago. Although no one knows the specifics, we can speculate that some Egyptian baker neglected to rush the typical gruel of grains and water into the oven before the dough had trapped some airborne wild yeast. Then, rather than waste the fermented mess, the baker perhaps threw it into a batch of fresh dough, only to find that the resulting loaf was lighter and higher.

The process of leavening has led the world's bakers to create thousands of different loaves throughout the ages, including one of today's most popular bread genres, pizza. Rustic loaves of flatbread baked with a scattering of herbs, cheese, sausages, and other flavorings, pizzas evolved into another wonderful edible invention, the calzone.

The name calzone comes from the Italian word for trousers, calze. Originally these stuffed breads were baked in long, narrow shapes and resembled baggy pants. Today they are more typically formed into half-moon shapes.

"Anything that can go on a pizza can go into a calzone or another stuffed bread," says Chef Peter Reinhart, one of the California Culinary Academy's expert baking instructors. The main consideration is to make the filling neither too dry, creating an unpalatable texture, nor too wet, resulting in a crust that's soggy and difficult to handle. It's not necessary to precook firmer vegetables, such as broccoli and red peppers, as long as they are cut into 1/4-inch cubes or smaller. Softer ingredients can be cut larger.

In stromboli, one of Reinhart's favorite stuffed breads, the filling is rolled up in the bread dough, jelly-roll fashion. It's named after Stromboli, a volcanic island off the west coast of Italy, because when you cut into it, a creamy mass of melted cheese, reminiscent of molten lava, oozes out.

Here are some chef's tricks to producing delicious stuffed breads:

- *Be sure to leave a $^1/2$-inch border of dough so that when you roll up stuffed bread, you can seal it firmly. Pinch the seam as tight as you can to keep the filling inside.*

- *If you prefer a thinner crust, bake the bread right after stuffing it. If you want a softer texture, let the filled loaf rise for about an hour before baking.*

- *It's best to bake denser stuffed breads, such as stromboli, at 350°F instead of 425° to 450°F, as you would pizza. Determining doneness takes some experience. Don't be fooled if the crust feels hard and crisp. This doesn't guarantee that the interior of the loaf is completely baked. Also, it's best not to cut into stromboli right away. Allow the bread to stand for a minimum of 20 minutes so the inside can finish baking.*

- *Any dough that works for pizza will work for calzoni and stromboli. Try the calzone and stromboli bread recipes in this chapter or use your favorite bread dough, omitting any sugar.*

Calzone

A calzone is a pizza formed into a turnover-like pie. The outside is pizza dough; the inside is cheese, filling, and sauce. From this simple concept many creative variations can be made using almost any of the wrap fillings in this book. The key to good calzoni is the dough. The following recipe is also an excellent dough for pizza and stromboli.

Each recipe makes enough dough for 4 medium-size, 6 individual, or 1 to 2 large calzoni.

Use any combination of the following fillings or any other filling you would like to try:

Your favorite pizza sauce

Freshly grated Parmesan or Romano cheese

Grated mozzarella, Monterey Jack, or provolone cheese

Roasted or fresh garlic

Chopped or sliced onions, mushrooms, peppers, artichoke hearts, or other vegetables

Fresh or dried herbs, such as basil, oregano, and parsley

Various meats and sausages

Best Calzone Dough

Makes about 2 pounds of dough,
enough for 2 large, 4 medium,
or 6 individual calzoni

This is Chef Peter Reinhart's
favorite recipe for calzoni.
For a more rustic version,
he sometimes substitutes
1/4 cup whole wheat flour for
1/4 cup of the bread flour. In
addition to this recipe, you
can also make calzoni with
the stromboli dough on
page 60. For a nice touch,
brush the top of each calzone
with extra virgin olive oil and
sprinkle with grated Parmesan
cheese when the calzone
comes out of the oven.

4 cups bread flour

2 teaspoons salt

*1 1/2 teaspoons instant yeast (or 2 teaspoons
active dry yeast dissolved in 1/4 cup
lukewarm water)*

3/4 cup cool water

1/2 cup milk

1/4 cup olive oil

1 teaspoon honey

*Egg wash (1 large egg whisked with
1 tablespoon cold water)*

In a large mixing bowl, stir together the flour, salt, and yeast. Stir in the water, milk, olive oil, and honey and beat until the mixture forms a ball. Turn the dough out onto a floured work surface and knead it for 10 minutes. You can also mix the dough using an electric mixer with a dough hook. It will take 5 to 8 minutes at medium speed to mix and knead the dough.

The dough should be stretchy and almost sticky. You should be able to stretch a small piece into a very thin, translucent membrane by pulling very slowly (this is called windowpaning; it tests the hydration and gluten development of the dough). If the dough seems too sticky, add a few more tablespoons of flour. If the dough tears easily, knead it a few minutes longer. If it seems stiff and tough, add a small amount of water.

Place the kneaded dough in a clean, lightly oiled bowl, cover with plastic wrap, and allow it to rise at room temperature for 90 minutes, or until doubled in size. Divide the dough into 2 to 6 pieces, shape them into balls, and let them rest, covered, in the refrigerator for at least 1 hour or until the next day.

When you're ready to bake the calzoni, preheat the oven to 450°F. Divide the dough into the desired number of pieces and roll out each piece on a lightly floured work surface into rounds about 1/4 inch thick. If you are making 2 large calzoni, roll each half of dough into a 12-inch-diameter round and fill with about 2 1/2 cups of sauce, filling, and cheese. For 4 medium calzoni, roll each piece of dough into a 9-inch-diameter round and fill with about 1 3/4 cups of sauce, filling, and cheese. For 6 individual calzoni, roll each piece of dough into a 6- to 7-inch-diameter round and fill with about 1 cup of sauce, filling, and cheese.

Cover the bottom half of each piece of dough with the sauce, filling, and cheese, leaving a 1/2-inch border of dough uncovered. Brush the uncovered edge of dough with the egg wash. Fold the top over, matching it with the bottom. Pinch or crimp the edge shut with your fingers or with a fork or crimping tool. Cut a small vent in the top. Brush the top with water or the egg.

Place the calzoni on a lightly oiled large baking sheet lined with baking parchment or on a pizza stone. Bake for 12 to 15 minutes (depending on the size), until the dough is golden brown, crisp, and puffy. (It will soften as it cools.) Allow the calzoni to cool for 5 minutes before serving.

Making Calzoni

On a lightly floured surface, roll out the dough in a circular shape about 1/4 inch thick. Cover half of the dough with sauce, if desired, leaving a 1/2-inch border of dough uncovered.

Top with the desired fillings, such as minced garlic, sliced mushrooms, olives, pepperoni, and shredded cheese.

Lift the uncovered half of the dough over the filling, matching the edges.

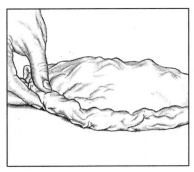

Press the edges together and crimp them.

Cut 2 or 3 vent holes in the top of the dough.

Red Potato and Broccoli Stuffed Calzone

Makes about 4¹/2 cups, enough
to fill 6 individual calzoni

To give your calzoni authentic
texture and a crisp bottom
crust, bake them on a pizza
stone. If you don't have one,
improvise by laying some flat,
unglazed ceramic floor tiles
on the oven rack.

3/4 pound red potatoes (about 6 small)

1/2 pound broccoli florets (about 1¹/2 cups)

*6 strips (1/4 pound) smoked bacon,
   if desired*

1 medium onion, coarsely chopped

6 cloves garlic, finely chopped

1/2 cup finely chopped fresh basil

1/4 cup freshly grated Parmesan cheese

1 tablespoon extra virgin olive oil

About 2 teaspoons salt

*1 teaspoon freshly ground black pepper,
   or to taste*

3/4 cup sour cream

1/4 cup finely chopped chives

1 recipe Best Calzone Dough (page 52)

*1¹/2 cups grated extra-sharp white cheddar
   cheese*

*Egg wash (1 large egg whisked with
   1 tablespoon cold water)*

Place the potatoes in a medium saucepan and add water to cover. Cook over medium-high heat just until tender, 15 to 20 minutes. Drain the potatoes and set them aside to cool, or plunge them into cold water to cool them faster. When the potatoes are cool enough to handle, cut them into thin slices.

In a small saucepan with a steamer basket, place 1 inch of water. Bring the water to a boil and steam the broccoli florets for about 4 minutes, or just until tender. After steaming, immediately plunge the broccoli into cold water to stop the cooking. Drain and set aside.

In a frying pan, cook the bacon until crisp. Drain the strips on paper towels and set aside.

In a large bowl, combine the potatoes with the broccoli, bacon, onion, garlic, basil, and cheese. Add the olive oil, salt, and pepper and gently stir to combine the ingredients. In a small bowl, blend the sour cream and chopped chives and set aside.

Preheat the oven to 450°F. Divide the calzone dough into 6 equal pieces and let the pieces rest for 5 minutes on a lightly floured surface. Roll each piece out into an 8-inch-diameter round. Spread 2 tablespoons of the sour cream mixture on each dough circle, leaving a 1/2-inch border uncovered. Place a heaping 3/4 cup of the vegetable mixture on the bottom half of each dough round (keeping the 1/2-inch border uncovered). Top each vegetable mound with 1 slice crumbled bacon and 1/4 cup (2 ounces) cheddar cheese.

Brush the edges of the dough with the egg wash. Fold the empty half of the dough over the filled portion until the edges meet. Seal the edges carefully by pressing down along the length of the semicircular edge firmly with a fork.

Lightly oil 1 or 2 baking sheets or line with baking parchment. Place the calzoni about 2 inches apart on the sheet. (Alternatively, you can place the calzone on an untreated pizza stone.) Brush each calzone with the remaining egg wash, and cut 3 small vent holes on the top, if desired. Bake the calzoni for about 20 minutes, or until golden brown. Cool them for 5 minutes before serving.

Note Reheat leftover calzoni on a lightly oiled or parchment-lined sheet or on a pizza stone for about 10 minutes in a preheated 350°F oven.

Sautéed Chicken and Mediterranean Vegetable Stuffed Calzone

Makes 4½ cups, enough to fill
6 individual calzoni

Fresh oregano, spicy
peperoncini, piquant
Kalamata olives, and tangy
bits of artichoke hearts
and feta cheese give a
Mediterranean flavor to this
hearty chicken filling.

1 whole boneless, skinless chicken breast
(about ½ pound)

MARINADE

2 tablespoons extra virgin olive oil

1 tablespoon dry white wine or lemon juice

3 cloves garlic, finely chopped

2 teaspoons chopped fresh oregano
or 1 teaspoon dried

½ teaspoon salt

½ teaspoon freshly ground black pepper

1 bay leaf

FILLING

¾ cup chopped pitted Kalamata olives

¾ cup diced marinated artichoke hearts

¾ cup drained peperoncini, stems removed,
cut into ⅛-inch-thick rings

¾ cup chopped oil-marinated dried
tomatoes

½ cup (3 ounces) crumbled feta cheese
or other grated cheese

2 tablespoons extra virgin olive oil

1 tablespoon dry white wine or juice
of 1 lemon

1 tablespoon chopped fresh parsley

2 teaspoons chopped fresh oregano
or 1 teaspoon dried

½ teaspoon salt, or to taste

¼ teaspoon freshly ground black pepper,
or to taste

WRAPPER

1 recipe Best Calzone Dough (page 52)

Egg wash (1 large egg whisked with
1 tablespoon cold water)

Rinse the chicken breast and pat it dry. Cut the chicken breast in half lengthwise, then slice across the grain into ⅛-inch-wide strips. Place the chicken strips in a small glass or other nonreactive bowl.

Prepare the marinade: In a large bowl, combine all the marinade ingredients. Pour the marinade over the chicken and refrigerate for at least 30 minutes or up to 4 hours.

Heat a large frying pan over medium-high heat. Add the chicken and marinade and cook, stirring occasionally, for about 2 minutes, until the chicken is no longer pink. Remove the chicken from the pan with a slotted spoon and set it aside. Discard the marinade.

Prepare the filling: In a large glass bowl, combine all the filling ingredients. Stir in the chicken.

Preheat the oven to 450°F. Divide the dough into 6 equal pieces and let the pieces rest for 5 minutes on a lightly floured surface. Roll each piece out into an 8-inch-diameter round. Place ¾ cup of the chicken filling on the bottom half of each round, leaving a ½-inch border uncovered. Brush the edges of the dough with the egg wash. Fold the empty half of the dough over the filled portion until the edges meet. Seal the edges carefully by pressing down along the length of the semicircular edge firmly with a fork.

Lightly oil 1 or 2 baking sheets or line with baking parchment. Place the calzoni about 2 inches apart on the sheet. (Alternatively, you can place the calzone on an untreated pizza stone.) Brush each calzone with the remaining egg wash and cut 3 small vent holes on the top. Bake the calzoni for 18 to 20 minutes, or until golden brown. Cool for 5 minutes before serving.

Note Reheat leftover calzoni on a lightly oiled or parchment-lined sheet or on a pizza stone for about 10 minutes in a preheated 350°F oven.

Roast Vegetable and
Goat Cheese Calzone

**Makes about 5¹/2 cups, enough
to fill 6 individual calzoni**

These calzoni burst with a
kaleidoscope of colors and
the sunny flavors of Italy—
of melted tangy goat and
smoked gouda cheeses.

1 eggplant (about 12 ounces)

1 small red bell pepper

1 small yellow bell pepper

1 small green bell pepper

6 Roma or plum tomatoes

1 small red onion

1 whole bulb garlic, separated into cloves
   (leave peels on)

1/3 cup fruity olive oil

5 sprigs thyme

2 teaspoons salt, or to taste

1 teaspoon freshly ground black pepper,
   or to taste

3/4 cup (6 ounces) soft goat cheese, ricotta,
   or mascarpone

1 tablespoon chopped fresh parsley

1/8 teaspoon freshly grated nutmeg

1 egg

6 tablespoons freshly grated Parmesan cheese

6 ounces smoked mozzarella, smoked
   gouda, fontina, or provolone cheese,
   cut into 6 slices

WRAPPER

1 recipe Best Calzone Dough (page 52)

Egg wash (1 large egg whisked with
   1 tablespoon cold water)

Preheat the oven to 425°F. Cut the eggplant lengthwise into 1/4-inch-thick slices. Then cut the slices into 1/2-inch-wide strips. Seed the peppers and cut the flesh into 1/2-inch-wide strips. Cut the tomatoes into 1/4-inch-thick slices. Cut the onion into 1/2-inch-thick slices.

In a large glass or nonreactive baking dish, toss the vegetables with the garlic cloves, the olive oil, the thyme, salt, and pepper. Bake for 45 minutes to 1 hour. Stir the mixture several times during the cooking and remove it from the oven when the vegetables are soft and the eggplant is lightly browned. Let the vegetables cool slightly, then place all except the garlic in a bowl. Squeeze the softened garlic cloves out from their papery peels and place them in the bowl with the vegetables. Discard the peels. Remove the sprigs of thyme and discard.

In a small bowl, combine the goat cheese, parsley, nutmeg, and egg and mix well.

Divide the calzone dough into 6 equal pieces and let them rest for 5 minutes on lightly floured surface. Roll each piece into an 8-inch-diameter round. Place a heaping 1/3 cup of the vegetable mixture on the bottom half of each round, leaving a 1/2-inch border uncovered. Spoon 2 tablespoons of the goat cheese mixture on top of the vegetables and top with another heaping 1/3 cup of vegetables. Top each vegetable mound with a tablespoon of Parmesan cheese and a 1-ounce slice of smoked mozzarella. Brush the edges of the dough with the egg wash.

Fold the empty half of the dough over the filled portion until the edges meet. Seal the edges carefully by pressing down along the length of the semi-circular edge firmly with a fork.

Lightly oil 1 or 2 baking sheets or line with baking parchment. Place the calzoni about 2 inches apart on the sheet. (Alternatively, you can place the calzone on an untreated pizza stone.) Brush each calzone with the remaining egg wash and cut 3 small vent holes on the top. Bake the calzoni for about 20 minutes, or until golden brown. Cool for 5 minutes before serving. (See also calzone baking instructions for Best Calzone Dough on p. 52.)

Note Reheat leftover calzoni on a lightly oiled or parchment-lined sheet or on a pizza stone for about 10 minutes in a preheated 350°F oven.

Stromboli

A stromboli is a filled or stuffed bread wrap that's made like a pizza and then rolled up like a jelly roll rather than folded in half like a calzone. Stromboli are usually baked as a whole loaf, then sliced for serving. For an interesting variation, try slicing the loaf before baking it. These small pinwheel slices are called strombolini or little stromboli.

Stromboli are very popular in the eastern United States, where they are usually made with pizza dough and stuffed with cheese fillings.

The technique for making stromboli is simple. Roll out your favorite bread or pizza dough into a rectangular shape about 1/4 inch thick. Then cover it with grated cheese and other fillings, roll it up, and bake. The following recipe is one variation, made interesting by the use of spices and polenta in the dough.

There are unlimited possibilities for fillings. Here are some of Chef Reinhart's favorite ideas:

Basil pesto, diced dried tomatoes, sliced olives, sautéed onions and mushrooms, and a combination of shredded cheeses

Gorgonzola, toasted walnuts, and caramelized onions

Roasted red peppers, minced garlic, and chopped fresh herbs such as oregano, thyme, and parsley

Smoked chicken or chicken sausage, diced dried tomatoes, grated Parmesan, and provolone

Diced cooked potatoes, crumbled cooked bacon, and fresh rosemary

Sautéed spinach, mustard greens, and red onions; prosciutto; and pine nuts

Making Stromboli

On a lightly floured surface, roll out the dough into a rectangular shape about 1/4 inch thick.

Sprinkle the filling ingredients over the dough, leaving a 1/2-inch border.

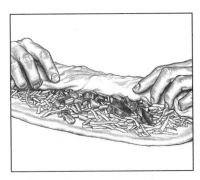

Starting from one of the longer sides, roll up the dough into a tight roll.

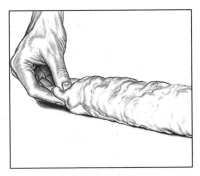

Pinch the ends and bottom seam closed and place the dough, seam side down, on a baking sheet.

Peppery Polenta Stromboli

**Makes 2 stromboli,
6 to 8 servings**

DOUGH

6 cups bread flour

1/4 cup coarsely ground cornmeal

1 tablespoon instant yeast (or
4 teaspoons active dry yeast
dissolved in 1/3 cup lukewarm
water)

1 tablespoon salt

1 teaspoon whole fennel seeds

1/2 teaspoon freshly ground black pepper

1/4 cup olive oil

About 2 cups water, at room
temperature

FILLING

2 tablespoons olive oil

1 onion, chopped

1 large red bell pepper, seeded and
coarsely chopped, or 1 cup chopped
roasted red peppers

1/2 cup sliced shiitake or white mushrooms

3 cloves garlic, minced

1/2 cup chopped green or black olives

1/2 cup chopped marinated artichoke hearts

1 cup grated cheddar cheese

1 cup grated mozzarella or Monterey
Jack cheese

Make the dough: In a large mixing bowl, combine the flour, cornmeal, yeast, salt, fennel seeds, and pepper. Add the oil and most of the water (reserve a little water until you need it). Stir the ingredients until the mixture forms a ball. Turn the ball of dough out onto a lightly floured work surface and knead it for 10 minutes. Add water or flour as needed; the dough should be soft, stretchy, and tacky but not sticky. If it seems stiff and dense, work in more water until it opens up. After kneading, you should be able to stretch out a small piece, pulling slowly and gently, until it is translucent and thin as a membrane (this is called windowpaning, and it tests whether the gluten protein is properly hydrated and developed). You can also make the dough in an electric mixer fitted with a dough hook. Combine all the ingredients and mix at medium speed for 5 to 8 minutes, until the dough is soft and stretchy as described above.

Place the dough in a clean, lightly oiled bowl, cover it with plastic wrap, and allow the dough to rise at room temperature for 1 1/2 hours, until doubled in size.

Make the filling: Heat the olive oil in a large frying pan over high heat. Add the onion and cook until it is translucent, about 5 minutes. Stir in the pepper and mushrooms and continue cooking until the vegetables begin to soften. Then add the garlic, olives, and artichoke hearts. Remove the mixture from the heat and let cool.

Prepare a baking sheet by lightly spraying or wiping it with oil (or line it with baking parchment). Sprinkle with a small amount of cornmeal or gritty semolina flour.

Preheat the oven to 350°F. Divide the dough in half and roll each half into a 12×8-inch rectangle that is about 1/4 inch thick. The dough may fight you and try to spring back to the center. If so, let it rest about 3 minutes to relax the gluten. Then roll again, working from the center out. It may take several attempts to get it rolled out all the way.

Sprinkle half of the vegetable filling evenly over the entire surface of the dough, leaving a 1/2-inch border uncovered. Sprinkle on half of the cheeses.

Starting from one of the longer edges, carefully roll the dough into a tight log. If any of the filling falls out, simply push it back in. Pinch the ends and the bottom seam closed. Place the dough seam side down on the baking sheet.

Bake the stromboli immediately for a thin crust, or set it aside to rise for 1 hour for a breadier loaf. Bake the stromboli for 35 to 45 minutes, until the dough is golden brown and sounds hollow when tapped. Turn off the oven and allow the stromboli to remain in it for an additional 15 minutes. Remove it and let it stand for another 10 minutes before serving. You can also allow the stromboli to cool completely and serve it later cold.

Making Strombolini

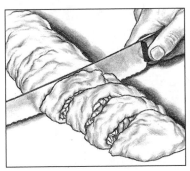

Cut the filled and rolled stromboli into 1-inch-thick portions.

Peel each piece off the loaf and lay it on a baking sheet, cut side up.

Note For a variation, called strombolini, cut the filled and rolled stromboli into 1-inch-thick slices before baking. Lay each slice cut side up (as you would cinnamon buns) on the baking sheet. They will look like pinwheels. Sprinkle the top of each pinwheel with a little dried parsley. (Fresh parsley may get too brown.) Allow to rise for 1 hour, then bake for 25 to 30 minutes.

You can also make smaller cocktail-size stromboli or strombolini by dividing the stromboli dough into quarters and rolling out each piece of the dough into an 8×4-inch rectangle.

Basic Crêpe Batter

Cheese Blintzes

Breton Buckwheat Crêpes with
Grilled Beef, Apples, and Blue Cheese

Pesto Crêpes with Roasted
Ratatouille

Apple Crêpes

Chocolate Crêpes

Chocolate Crème Fraîche

Raspberry Soufflé Crêpes

Crêpes

Crêpes are as international as they are versatile. While most people associate crêpes with Brittany because of the *crêperies* that line nearly every street in that northwestern French province, these thin filled pancakes are popular all over the world.

Hungarian *palacsinta*, Dutch *pannekoeken*, Jewish *blintz*, and Italian *crespelle* are all variations of the classic French crêpe. Other unusual crêpes of the world include the *dosa* of southern India, a crisp "wrap" made from a frothy thin batter of fermented rice and white lentils, and *injera*, a spongy flat wrap from Ethiopia. Crêpe batters are easy to use and cook. They rely on a simple and flexible blend of flour, liquid (usually milk), and eggs.

Once you develop a feel for the consistency of the batter—thin enough to swirl quickly across the crêpe pan, but thick enough to handle and wrap—it's easy to play with other flours or to replace the milk with yogurt, fruit or vegetable purees, or a well-seasoned stock.

The rule of thumb when adding yogurt, a puree, or stock is to begin with $1/2$ cup per cup of flour (with 2 eggs). Blend well and let the mixture rest for 30 minutes. Then whisk in some more (or a little milk), a tablespoon at a time, until the proper texture is achieved.

Vary the type of flour. Try using all buckwheat flour in place of white flour or experiment with the following flours mixed half and half with white flour: garbanzo, whole wheat, semolina, rice, quinoa, blue corn, or potato starch.

Nonfat egg substitutes can be used ($1/4$ cup for each egg called for), as well as vegetarian egg replacers.

Your favorite liqueurs, herbs, ground spices, or other natural flavors and colors can be incorporated. Coloring and flavoring crêpes can be as simple as adding a teaspoon of turmeric, a few strands of saffron, or a table-spoon or two of paprika. Or it can be as exotic as using a few ink sacs from fresh squid to make elegant black crêpes, perfect for stuffing with seafood. Replace some of the milk with a berry puree—blueberries, raspberries, or strawberries buzzed in a blender with a little sugar and lemon juice. Beets, dried tomatoes, and spinach are just a few of the vegetables that can be pureed for delicious flavor and color.

Crêpes are great any time of day. For breakfast, try crêpes spread with fruit preserves or stuffed with sautéed apples. Pesto-flavored crêpes sprinkled with grated Parmesan cheese or buckwheat crêpes filled with thin slices of ham and Gruyère cheese make ideal snacks. Crêpes filled with grilled beef and blue cheese or roasted ratatouille are terrific entrées. For dessert, try chocolate crêpes rolled around a silky chocolate crème fraîche or blintzes filled with lemon curd and raspberries or with fresh mango, mascarpone, and toasted coconut.

Basic Crêpe Batter

3 eggs
2 tablespoons sugar (omit for savory crêpes)
1 1/2 teaspoons salt
2 cups milk

2 cups all-purpose flour
2 tablespoons melted butter, plus extra for
the pan
Additional milk or water

**Makes 24 to 36 crêpes,
depending on size of pan**

In a bowl, whisk together the eggs, sugar, and salt. Add the milk, blending well. Then add the flour, whisking until the mixture is smooth. Fold in the melted butter, cover the bowl, and refrigerate the batter for at least 1 hour, preferably overnight.

Heat a 6- to 8-inch, preferably nonstick crêpe pan or other medium-weight, curve-sided pan over medium-high heat. With a paper towel, lightly grease the pan with melted butter or lightly spray it with nonstick pan spray. The pan should be hot enough so that a drop of water will skitter across it and disappear quickly.

Using a small ladle or big spoon, ladle several tablespoons of batter into the center of the hot pan, tilting and swirling the pan as you pour until the batter covers the bottom. Pour off any excess batter. Cook the crêpe for about 30 seconds, or until the edges curl and the bottom lightly browns. Lift the edge with a spatula, then, using the spatula or your fingers, gently flip the crêpe and cook the other side for 30 seconds, or until lightly browned. Remove the crêpe from the pan and stack it on a plate. Repeat with the remaining batter. If the batter becomes too thick, thin it with a small amount of water. Fill as desired.

For variety, add other flavors to this basic crêpe recipe. For dessert crêpes, for example, fold in 3 ounces of grated chocolate or 1 ounce of Frangelico or Grand Marnier, a tablespoon of vanilla or almond extract, or grated lemon zest. For savory crêpes, try adding a tablespoon of snipped fresh chives, dill, or chopped basil. Or create your own flavor combinations.

Ideally the batter will just coat a spoon. You may need to add some extra liquid if the batter thickens during the standing period. A chef's trick for light crêpes is to thin the batter with carbonated soda or mineral water.

Cheese Blintzes

Makes 24 blintzes

These thin pancakes, bursting with a creamy cheese filling, are remarkably versatile. Garnish them with your favorite fruit preserves, puree, or syrup or with fresh seasonal berries, lemon curd, or applesauce. Or simply serve them with a dollop of sour cream or crème fraîche and a sprinkling of cinnamon sugar. Still other possibilities: Fold 1/2 cup of sour cherries, strawberries, blueberries, or diced fresh mango into the cheese mixture. Fresh mango blintzes are delicious garnished with mascarpone and toasted shredded coconut.

For blintzes, the crepes or thin pancakes are cooked on only one side. They are filled with a sweetened cheese mixture, browned in sizzling butter until golden, and

BLINTZES
1 1/4 cups milk
5 eggs
1 tablespoon melted butter or canola oil
1/2 teaspoon salt
1 1/4 cups all-purpose flour

CHEESE FILLING
1 1/2 pounds (3 cups) ricotta or farmer's cheese (see note on page 69)

1 egg plus 1 egg yolk
1 tablespoon plus 1 teaspoon sugar
1 1/2 teaspoons ground cinnamon
1 1/2 teaspoons vanilla extract
1 teaspoon grated lemon or orange zest

1 tablespoon melted butter or nonstick pan spray

Make the blintzes: In a large bowl, whisk together the milk, eggs, melted butter, and salt. Then add the flour, whisking until the mixture is smooth. Cover and refrigerate the batter for 1 hour. If necessary, when you are ready to cook the blintzes, thin the batter with additional milk, water, or carbonated water, until it is just thick enough to coat a spoon.

Heat a 6- to 8-inch, preferably nonstick crêpe pan or other medium-weight, curve-sided pan over medium-high heat. With a paper towel, lightly grease the pan with melted butter or lightly spray it with nonstick pan spray. The pan should be hot enough so that a drop of water will skitter across it and disappear quickly.

Using a small ladle or big spoon, ladle several tablespoons of batter into the center of the hot pan, tilting and swirling the pan as you pour until the batter covers the bottom. Cook the blintz for about 30 seconds, or until the edges curl and the bottom lightly browns. Remove the blintz from the pan and stack it on a plate. Repeat with the remaining batter. If the batter becomes too thick, thin it with a small amount of water.

Prepare the filling: In a bowl, combine the cheese, eggs, sugar, cinnamon, vanilla, and lemon zest, blending well. Place a rounded tablespoon of filling in the center of the browned side of each blintz. Fold the left and right sides about an inch over the filling. Then fold in the top and bottom sides, enclosing the filling and forming a rectangular envelope.

Cook the blintzes: Melt the butter in a large frying pan. Add the blintzes in a single layer and cook about 3 minutes per side, until golden brown and heated through. You may have to cook them in several batches. If so, arrange the cooked blintzes in a single layer on a baking sheet and keep them warm for up to 30 minutes in a 250°F oven. If you are not serving them right away, cover the pan with aluminum foil to prevent them from drying out.

served hot. If you want to save a few calories, arrange the filled blintzes on a baking sheet lightly coated with melted butter or nonstick pan spray and bake them in a 400°F oven for about 10 minutes, or until lightly browned and heated through.

To save time, make the pancakes ahead of time, only cooking them on one side. Cool them completely before stacking them, browned side up. Then wrap the stack in plastic wrap or aluminum foil and refrigerate for up to 5 days or freeze for up to 2 months.

Note You can substitute 1 pound small-curd cottage cheese for the ricotta cheese. Drain the cottage cheese in a strainer for at least 1 hour or overnight in the refrigerator. Press it through a sieve before using.

Breton Buckwheat Crêpes with Grilled Beef, Apples, and Blue Cheese

Makes 12 to 16 crêpes, 6 to 8 entrée servings

What a wonderful discovery to find that you can use buckwheat flour by itself to produce nutty-flavored crêpes. If you wish for a more delicate flavor, substitute all-purpose flour for half of the buckwheat flour. As with nearly all recipes, use fresh herbs whenever possible.

This is a good recipe to remember next time you have leftover grilled rib-eye, tenderloin, or sirloin steak. Just slice the beef into thin strips and add it to the savory apple and cheese filling.

For another delicious and quick entrée, wrap thinly sliced baked ham and Gruyère cheese in these buckwheat crêpes. Bake them in a warm oven just until the cheese melts.

CRÊPES

1 cup nonfat yogurt or buttermilk

2 eggs or 1/2 cup egg substitute

1 teaspoon olive oil

1 1/3 cups buckwheat flour (or blend of buckwheat and all-purpose)

3/4 teaspoon salt

About 1/2 cup sparkling apple cider

FILLING

1 1/2 pounds 1-inch-thick rib-eye, sirloin, or tenderloin steaks, pounded slightly

1 cup sparkling apple cider

1 tablespoon olive oil

1 teaspoon finely chopped fresh sage or 1/2 teaspoon dried

1 teaspoon finely chopped fresh rosemary or 1/2 teaspoon dried

1 teaspoon finely chopped fresh thyme or 1/2 teaspoon dried

2 tart apples, cored and thinly sliced

1 large red onion, sliced 1/2 inch thick

Salt and pepper to taste

8 ounces blue cheese, crumbled

1 cup beef stock

Prepare the crêpes: In a bowl, whisk together the yogurt, eggs, and olive oil. Whisk in the buckwheat flour and salt until very smooth. Whisk in about 1/2 cup cider, 1 tablespoon at a time, to form a batter just thick enough to coat a spoon. Cover and refrigerate for at least 1 hour, preferably overnight.

Prepare the filling: In a bowl, toss the steak with the cider, olive oil, sage, rosemary, thyme, apples, onion, salt, pepper, and 1 tablespoon of the blue cheese. Cover and refrigerate for at least 1 hour.

Heat a 10-inch crêpe pan or other medium-weight, curve-sided pan over medium-high heat. With a paper towel, lightly grease the pan with melted butter or lightly spray it with nonstick pan spray. The pan should be hot enough so that a drop of water will skitter across it and disappear quickly.

Using a small ladle or big spoon, ladle several tablespoons of batter into the center of the hot pan, tilting and swirling pan as you pour until the batter covers the bottom. Cook the crêpe for about 30 seconds, or until the edges curl and the bottom lightly browns. Lift the edge with a spatula, then, using the spatula or your fingers, gently flip the crêpe and cook the other side for about 30 seconds, or until lightly browned. Remove the crêpe from the pan and stack it on a plate. Repeat with the remaining batter. If the batter becomes too thick, thin it with a small amount of sparkling cider or water.

Preheat the broiler or grill. Drain the steak, apple, and onion, reserving the marinade. Broil or grill the steak, turning once, until it is medium rare, 8 to 10 minutes. Let cool. Broil or grill the apple slices and onions until they are lightly marked and slightly softened, about 5 minutes. Thinly slice the steak and toss the pieces in a bowl with the apples, onion, and remaining cheese.

Preheat the oven to 375°F. Roll about $1/4$ cup of the steak mixture in each crêpe, place the crêpes on a lightly buttered or sprayed baking sheet, and bake them for about 10 minutes, or until lightly browned.

In a saucepan, bring the reserved marinade and beef stock to a vigorous boil, then reduce the heat to a simmer. Cook about 5 minutes, or until the sauce thickens slightly. Drizzle the sauce on the crêpes just before serving.

Pesto Crêpes with Roasted Ratatouille

Makes 12 to 16 crêpes

Pesto-flavored crêpes make great snacks. Simply sprinkle a warm crêpe with some grated Parmesan cheese and roll it up. Or embellish it by adding some thin strips of roasted red pepper or diced fresh tomatoes.

To save time, you can use 1 cup prepared pesto. Add one-third of the pesto to the crêpe batter and reserve the rest for topping the crêpes. You may also want to garnish crêpes with a spoonful of warm marinara or tomato sauce.

CRÊPES

1 cup milk

2 eggs or $1/4$ cup egg substitute

$1/2$ cup semolina or garbanzo flour

$1/2$ cup all-purpose flour

$1/2$ teaspoon salt

PESTO

6 tablespoons olive oil

6 cloves garlic

1 cup fresh parsley leaves

$1/4$ cup pine nuts or walnuts

$1/4$ cup grated Parmesan or Romano cheese

1 cup fresh basil leaves

Juice of $1/2$ lemon

$1/4$ teaspoon salt

Freshly ground black pepper to taste

ROASTED RATATOUILLE

1 eggplant (about $3/4$ pound), cut lengthwise in half, then thinly sliced

2 zucchini, cut lengthwise in half, then thinly sliced

2 tomatoes, peeled, seeded, and coarsely chopped, or $1 1/2$ cups drained and chopped canned tomatoes

2 tablespoons olive oil

1 tablespoon finely chopped fresh oregano or $1 1/2$ teaspoons dried

$1/2$ teaspoon salt

Freshly ground black pepper to taste

$1/4$ cup grated Parmesan or Romano cheese

$1/2$ cup ricotta cheese (optional)

Prepare the crêpe batter: In a bowl, whisk together the milk, eggs, semolina, flour, and salt until the mixture is very smooth.

In a food processor, combine 4 tablespoons of the olive oil and the garlic, parsley, pine nuts, and Parmesan; pulse until smooth. Whisk $1/3$ cup of this mixture into the crêpe batter and refrigerate the batter for at least 1 hour. Add the basil, lemon juice, salt, pepper, and remaining 2 tablespoons olive oil to the remaining parsley mixture and pulse several times, or until the pesto is the desired smoothness. Refrigerate the pesto until ready to use.

Prepare the ratatouille: Preheat the oven to 425°F. Lightly oil a large stainless steel, ceramic, or glass baking dish. Layer the dish with the eggplant and zucchini. Sprinkle the tomatoes, olive oil, oregano, salt, and pepper on top and bake for 20 to 30 minutes, until the vegetables soften and are lightly browned. Leave the oven on.

Make the crêpes: While the vegetables are roasting, heat a 10-inch crêpe pan or other medium-weight, curve-sided pan over medium-high heat. With a paper towel, lightly grease the pan with melted butter or lightly spray it with nonstick pan spray. The pan should be hot enough so that a drop of water will skitter across it and disappear quickly.

Using a small ladle or big spoon, ladle several tablespoons of batter into the center of the hot pan, tilting and swirling the pan as you pour until a thin layer of batter covers the bottom. Cook the crêpe for about 30 seconds, or until the edges curl and the bottom lightly browns. Lift the edge with a spatula, then, using the spatula or your fingers, gently flip the crêpe and cook the other side for 30 seconds, or until lightly browned. Remove the crêpe from the pan and stack it on a plate. Repeat with the remaining batter.

Fold the Parmesan and ricotta into the vegetables. Roll about $1/3$ cup of the ratatouille into each crêpe. When all of the crêpes are filled, place them on an oiled baking sheet and bake for about 6 minutes, until they are slightly crisp and heated through. Spoon the pesto on the crêpes just before serving.

Note If desired, roast the vegetables ahead of time and refrigerate them. Bring them to room temperature before filling the crêpes. Increase the final baking time to about 10 minutes or bake the crêpes until they are lightly browned and the filling is heated through.

Apple Crêpes

Makes 5 servings

Serve these elegant yet homey crêpes for brunch as well as for dinner. If you want to be fancier, place a scoop of vanilla ice cream and a splash of warm caramel sauce alongside the warm crêpes.

If desired, soften the raisins in a few tablespoons of warm Calvados or brandy. Add the brandy to the filling.

2 tablespoons butter

2 large or 3 to 4 medium Golden Delicious, Granny Smith, or Pippin apples, peeled, cored, and cut into small cubes (about 2 cups)

2 tablespoons granulated sugar

1 tablespoon firmly packed brown sugar

2 tablespoons raisins, soaked in hot water, then drained

1 teaspoon vanilla extract

1 teaspoon ground cinnamon

1/4 teaspoon ground cloves

1/3 cup walnuts or pecans, toasted

10 crêpes, about 6 inches in diameter (see Basic Crêpe Batter recipe, page 67)

1 cup crème fraîche or sour cream

Melt the butter in large frying pan over medium-high heat. Add the apples, granulated sugar, brown sugar, raisins, vanilla, cinnamon, and cloves, stirring until combined. Cook the mixture over medium heat, stirring occasionally, until the apples are tender and the sauce thickens, about 5 minutes.

Place 1 rounded tablespoon of apple mixture and 1 teaspoon of chopped walnuts in the center of each crêpe. Fold the left and right sides to the center over the filling, then fold up from the edge closest to you. Serve the crêpes on individual plates, garnished with a dollop of crème fraîche and a sprinkling of the remaining walnuts.

Chocolate Crêpes

2 cups milk
3 ounces grated semisweet chocolate
  (1/2 cup semisweet chocolate chips)
3 eggs

2 tablespoons sugar
1 1/2 teaspoons salt
2 cups all-purpose or white pastry flour
2 tablespoons melted butter

Makes 30 crêpes

Delicately flavored chocolate crêpes lend themselves to many fillings: raspberry or apricot soufflé, creamy chocolate crème fraîche, semisoft ice cream, or fresh berries, to name just a few.

In a saucepan, bring the milk to a boil. Place the chocolate in a bowl, pour the milk over it, and stir until the chocolate is completely incorporated.

In a separate bowl, whisk together the eggs, sugar, and salt. Slowly whisk in the warm chocolate, stirring until the mixture is completely blended. Add the flour and melted butter and whisk until the batter is smooth. Cover the bowl and refrigerate the batter for at least an hour. If necessary, thin the batter with milk or water before making the crêpes.

Heat a 6- to 8-inch, preferably nonstick crêpe pan or other medium-weight curve-sided pan over medium-high heat. Brush it lightly with melted butter. Spoon about 2 1/2 tablespoons of the batter into the center of the pan and tilt and swirl the pan until a thin layer of batter covers the bottom. Cook the crêpe for about 30 seconds, until the bottom is lightly browned. Lift the edge with a spatula, then, using the spatula or your fingers, flip the crêpe and lightly brown the second side, about 30 seconds.

Turn the crêpe out on parchment or wax paper and cool. Repeat with the remaining batter. Fill as desired.

Chocolate Crème Fraîche

Makes about 2¹/2 cups

Chocolate lovers will rejoice
when they taste this silky-
textured, pudding-like filling.

2 cups heavy cream
8 ounces semisweet chocolate, grated,
   or semisweet chocolate chips
2 tablespoons buttermilk

2 tablespoons sugar (optional)
¹/2 teaspoon vanilla extract

In a saucepan, heat the cream to the scalding point (just below boiling).
Place the chocolate in a heatproof bowl. Pour the cream over the chocolate and
stir until the chocolate is completely melted and the mixture is smooth. Stir in
the buttermilk and combine it thoroughly. Cover the bowl with cheesecloth
and let it stand in a warm part of the kitchen for 12 to 24 hours, until the chocolate mixture has thickened. Refrigerate the mixture overnight.

Softly whip the chilled mixture, adding the sugar, if desired, and the
vanilla. Refrigerate until ready to use.

•

Raspberry Soufflé Crêpes

1/2 cup raspberry jam
1 tablespoon framboise
6 large egg whites
1/4 teaspoon cream of tartar

1/4 cup sugar
24 Chocolate Crêpes (follow recipe on page 75 but cook crêpes on one side only)

**Makes 12 servings,
2 crêpes per serving**

Preheat the oven to 350°F. In a bowl, blend together the raspberry jam and framboise. In a separate bowl, whip the egg whites and cream of tartar until the mixture is frothy. Gradually add the sugar while continuing to whip the egg whites until they form stiff, shiny peaks.

Gently stir 1/3 of the beaten egg whites into the raspberry mixture to lighten it. Then carefully fold in the remaining egg whites.

With the most attractive side on the outside, fold the crêpes in half and then in half again, forming a fan. Lift the top fold of the crêpe and place a heaping tablespoon of the soufflé mixture inside. Place the filled crêpes on a parchment-lined baking sheet. Bake them for 12 to 14 minutes, or until the soufflé has puffed nicely and is golden brown.

This is a very simple recipe that looks beautiful when plated with flourishes of raspberry coulis, a few fresh berries, and a light dusting of confectioners' sugar. To make the coulis, simply purée fresh or frozen raspberries and then press the mixture through a fine sieve. The tart sauce provides a nice complement to the sweet crêpes. A small amount of framboise, raspberry eau-de-vie, adds intense raspberry flavor to the airy filling.

Brie in Filo

Turkish Cheese "Cigarettes"

Lamb Appetizer Triangles

Wild Mushroom Filo Triangles

Sausage and Mushroom Filo Appetizers

Spinach Börek

Tuna and Egg Briks

Fresh Figs Wrapped in Cinnamon-Scented Filo

Ruby Poached Pears in Filo Nests with Chocolate Sauce

Bittersweet Chocolate Sauce

Apple Streusel Strudel

Filo

If you are ever invited to watch a strudel baker hand-stretch filo, don't hesitate to accept. It is rare to witness such culinary theater as expert hands deftly transform a small blob of high-gluten flour, water, and salt by stretching, flipping, twisting, and turning until it becomes as thin as parchment and wide enough to cover a large dining room table.

Unfortunately, filo making is becoming a lost art. Luckily, however, the machine-made dough tastes comparable to the handmade product.

Even though it is paper-thin, filo is easy to work with, as long as you protect it from drying out. Cover the sheets you are not using immediately with plastic wrap topped with a damp cloth, and you won't have a problem.

Throughout Europe, the Mediterranean, and the Middle East, filo is used for everything from the famous Moroccan *bisteeya*, a crisp golden brown "pie" of filo baked around shredded chicken, ground almonds, eggs, and exotic spices, to Greek *tiropetes*, bite-size cheese triangles; from Austrian strudel to Turkish *börek*, pastry packets filled with ground meat, spinach, or cheese.

Filo fits in perfectly with today's hectic lifestyles. It's readily available and is a lightweight alternative to rich puff pastry and pie dough. You need only the smallest amount of melted butter or oil to separate the layers.

Fold it to make Sausage and Mushroom Filo Appetizers; roll it for Turkish Cheese "Cigarettes" and Apple Streusel Strudel; twist it for Fresh Figs Wrapped in Cinnamon-Scented Filo; and use it as a wrapping for small wheels of Brie or last night's dinner. Filo gives leftovers new life.

Here are some tips:

- *Organize your* mise en place, *everything you need for the recipe, before you unwrap the package of filo.*
- *Use a light hand when you brush the sheets of filo with melted butter. You'll need about 2 teaspoons of butter per sheet. A 1 1/2- to 2 1/2-inch-wide natural bristle pastry brush or new paintbrush works well for quick buttering.*
- *Don't worry if your filo wrinkles, tears, or rips. Merely press the wrinkles flat, brush with melted butter and either patch the tear with a small piece of filo or cover it with a whole new sheet.*

Occasionally you can find fresh filo in Mediterranean markets or specialty food stores. However, frozen filo works well. It's best to thaw frozen filo slowly in the refrigerator. Filo is usually available in 1-pound packages of 24 sheets measuring about 18×12 inches. It has a generous shelf life, about 3 weeks well wrapped and refrigerated. Most foods wrapped in filo can be made in advance and held in the refrigerator for about 8 hours or in an airtight container in the freezer for several months.

Brie in Filo

1 round of Brie, no larger than 5 inches
    in diameter
5 sheets filo

$^1/_4$ cup ($^1/_2$ stick) butter, melted

Makes 6 to 8 servings

Preheat the oven to 375°F. On a clean work surface, lay a sheet of filo and brush it with butter. Place a second sheet of filo on top of the first and brush it with butter. Stack another sheet of filo on top and butter that. Continue until all the filo is buttered. Trim the filo to make a 12-inch square. Then trim off the corners, forming a circle.

Place the cheese in the center of the filo. Lift the edge of the filo and place it over the cheese. Continue lifting the filo, pleating it every inch or so, until you've completely enclosed the Brie. Brush the top of the filo with additional melted butter.

Place the enclosed Brie on a piece of aluminum foil with the edges turned up. Place the foil on a baking sheet and bake until the filo is golden brown, about 25 minutes. Serve while the cheese is still warm.

Brie baked in filo until the mellow cheese oozes out from underneath its crisp golden blanket is wonderful. Serve it as an appetizer or cheese course with a tart jam such as raspberry or cranberry relish, with crisp apple or pear slices, with crackers, or with salad greens.

Vary the flavor of this recipe by adding fresh or dried herbs, spices, or cracked pepper to the butter or by topping the Brie with pesto, dried tomatoes, roasted garlic, roasted peppers, or finely chopped walnuts or pecans sautéed in a small amount of melted butter. If you like, try Camembert, other soft-ripened cheeses, or small rounds of goat cheese instead of the Brie.

Turkish Cheese "Cigarettes"

These crisp filo sticks

make a lovely dessert or

teatime snack.

1 container (1 pound) ricotta or small-curd
   cottage cheese
2 eggs
1/4 cup sugar

$1/2$ teaspoon grated lemon zest
About 12 sheets filo
About $1/2$ cup (1 stick) butter, melted

Preheat the oven to 375°F. Combine the ricotta, eggs, sugar, and lemon zest.

Stack the sheets of filo on top of each other. With a sharp knife cut through all the sheets of filo lengthwise into thirds. Cover with plastic wrap topped with a damp cloth. Working with about 3 strips of filo at a time, place them parallel to each other with the narrow ends facing you. Brush the strips of filo with melted butter.

Place about 1 tablespoon of filling along the bottom edge of a filo strip, leaving a 1-inch border on both the right and left sides. Carefully roll up the filo, jelly roll style. If desired, pinch the ends together to contain the filling. Each filled pastry will measure approximately 4×1 inches. Place the filo rolls on a parchment-lined baking sheet. Repeat, using up the remaining filo and filling. (You should end up with about 36 "cigarettes.") Bake until the pastry is golden brown, about 15 minutes. Serve warm.

Lamb Appetizer Triangles

1 tablespoon olive or canola oil
1 small red onion, finely diced
    (about 1/2 cup)
1/2 red bell pepper, finely diced
    (about 1/2 cup)
1 cup finely diced cooked lamb
2 red-skinned potatoes, cooked and finely
    diced (about 1 cup)

1/4 cup mango chutney, coarsely
    chopped
1/2 teaspoon salt, or to taste
1/4 teaspoon freshly ground black pepper
9 sheets filo
About 1/3 cup melted butter or olive oil

Makes about 36 triangles

Here's a great idea for using leftover roast lamb. For an Indian flavor, add some curry powder and ground cumin to the filling.

Sweet-sour chutneys, made by simmering fruit with vinegar, sugar, and fragrant spices, are an essential condiment on Indian tables. One of the most popular and versatile is mango chutney; it's the perfect flavor booster for almost any sandwich, dip, or filling. Mango chutneys can be mild or spicy, smooth or chunky. The most widely available brands (such as Major Grey's) tend to be quite sweet and mild; explore an Indian market for other, intriguing versions.

Heat the oil in a frying pan over medium-high heat. Add the onion and bell pepper and sauté until the onion softens, about 5 minutes. In a bowl, combine the lamb, potatoes, chutney, salt, and black pepper with the sautéed onion and pepper.

Preheat the oven to 375°F. Stack the sheets of filo on top of each other and cut through the stack lengthwise into quarters. Stack the strips on top of one another and cover them with plastic wrap topped with a damp cloth. Place 4 or 5 strips at a time parallel to each other with the narrow ends closest to you. Lightly brush each strip with melted butter or oil. Place 1 tablespoon of filling on one end of each strip. Fold one corner over the filling to make a triangle. Fold the triangle over again on itself. Continue folding to the end as if you were folding a flag. Repeat with the rest of the filo and filling. Brush each triangle with melted butter.

Place the filled filo triangles on parchment-lined baking sheets, seam side down, and bake until they are golden brown, 12 to 15 minutes.

Wild Mushroom Filo Triangles

Makes 36 triangles

Baking wild mushrooms
in paper-thin layers of
crisp filo intensifies their
earthy flavor.

1 tablespoon olive oil

1 small onion, minced

12 ounces finely chopped wild mushrooms,
    such as chanterelles, morels, or
    portobellos (about 3 cups)

4 cloves garlic, minced

1/2 cup dry sherry

3/4 cup crumbled feta cheese

3/4 cup shredded mozzarella cheese

1/3 cup chopped fresh parsley

1 teaspoon salt

1 teaspoon finely chopped fresh oregano
    or 1/2 teaspoon dried

1 teaspoon finely chopped fresh thyme
    or 1/2 teaspoon dried

1/2 teaspoon freshly ground black pepper

9 sheets filo

1/2 cup (1 stick) butter, melted

Heat the oil in a large frying pan over medium-high heat. Add the onion
and sauté, stirring occasionally, until it becomes translucent, about 5 minutes.
Stir in the mushrooms, garlic, and sherry and cook until most of the liquid has
evaporated, about 5 minutes longer.

Remove the pan from the heat and stir in the feta, mozzarella, parsley,
salt, oregano, thyme, and pepper.

Preheat the oven to 375°F. Stack the sheets of filo on top of each other
and cut through the stack lengthwise into quarters. Stack the strips on top of
one another and cover them with plastic wrap topped with a damp cloth. Place
4 or 5 strips at a time parallel to each other with the narrow ends closest to you.
Lightly brush each strip with melted butter or oil. Place 1 tablespoon filling on
one end of each strip. Fold one corner over the filling to make a triangle. Fold
the triangle over again on itself. Continue folding to the end as if you were folding a flag. Try to keep the corners as tight as possible so the filling doesn't escape
during baking.

Place the filled triangles on parchment-lined baking sheets and bake
until golden brown, 12 to 15 minutes.

Sausage and Mushroom Filo Appetizers

1 tablespoon olive oil
1 small onion, cut in half and thinly sliced
2 cloves garlic, minced
1/2 pound mushrooms, minced
1 pound spicy Italian-style pork sausage

1 cup fresh or frozen peas
1 large ripe tomato, seeded and coarsely chopped
12 sheets filo
1/2 cup (1 stick) butter, melted

Makes about 48 appetizers

This flavorful filling also makes a great ravioli stuffing and is delightful served over pasta as a sauce.

Heat the oil in a large frying pan over medium-high heat. Add the onion and cook for about 5 minutes, until it becomes translucent. Add the garlic and mushrooms and cook, stirring, until most of the liquid has evaporated, about 5 minutes. Remove the vegetables from the pan to a mixing bowl.

In the same pan over medium-high heat, cook the sausage, stirring occasionally to break it up, until it is evenly browned, about 10 minutes. Drain off and discard the fat and add the sausage to the mixing bowl with the vegetables. Stir the peas and tomato into the mixture.

Preheat the oven to 375°F. Stack the sheets of filo on top of each other and cut through the stack lengthwise into quarters. Stack the strips on top of one another and cover them with plastic wrap topped with a damp cloth. Place 4 or 5 strips at a time parallel to each other with the narrow ends closest to you. Lightly brush each strip with melted butter or oil. Place 1 tablespoon of filling on one end of each strip. Fold one corner of filo over the filling to make a triangle. Fold the triangle over again on itself. Continue folding to the end as if you were folding a flag.

Place the filled triangles on parchment-lined baking sheets and bake until golden brown, about 12 minutes.

Spinach Börek

Makes about 48 triangles

These flaky, bite-size pastry triangles filled with spinach and cheese are popular throughout the Middle East. If you like, add chopped fresh dill, minced parsley, or even some freshly grated nutmeg to the filling.

1 package (10 ounces) frozen chopped spinach, thawed and squeezed dry

$1/2$ cup thinly sliced scallions, including tops (about 1 bunch)

$1/2$ pound feta cheese, crumbled (about 2 cups)

$1/4$ pound Monterey Jack cheese, shredded (1 cup)

$1/2$ cup ricotta or small-curd cottage cheese

$1/4$ teaspoon salt

$1/4$ teaspoon freshly ground black pepper

12 sheets filo

About $1/2$ cup melted butter or olive oil

Preheat the oven to 375°F. In a medium-size bowl, combine the spinach, scallions, feta, Monterey Jack, ricotta, salt, and pepper.

Stack the sheets of filo on top of each other and cut through the stack lengthwise into quarters. Stack the strips on top of one another and cover them with plastic wrap topped with a damp cloth. Place 4 or 5 strips at a time parallel to each other with the narrow ends closest to you. Lightly brush each strip with melted butter or oil. Place 1 tablespoon of filling on one end of each strip. Fold one corner of the filo over the filling to make a triangle. Fold the triangle over again on itself. Continue folding to the end as if you were folding a flag.

Place the filled triangles on parchment-lined baking sheets and bake until golden brown, 12 to 15 minutes.

Tuna and Egg Briks

1 tablespoon butter
1/2 small onion, minced (about 1/4 cup)
2 tablespoons minced red bell pepper
2 tablespoons minced fresh parsley
1 can (6 ounces) tuna packed in water,
    well drained

3 anchovy fillets, finely chopped
2 teaspoons capers
4 sheets filo
4 medium eggs
Oil for deep-frying

Makes 4 briks

Heat the butter in a small frying pan over medium-high heat. Add the onion and sauté until it becomes translucent, about 3 minutes. Stir in the bell pepper and parsley and cook 2 minutes longer. Remove the pan from the heat and stir in the tuna, anchovies, and capers. Let the mixture cool.

Place a sheet of filo with the longest side closest to you. Fold the filo in half, forming a rectangle measuring approximately 12 × 9 inches. Place 1/4 of the filling (about 1/4 cup) in the center of the filo. Form a hollow in the center of the filling and break an egg over it, depositing the yolk and most of the white in the hollow. Don't worry if the egg white isn't completely contained within the filling. Dip a pastry brush in the excess egg white and lightly brush it in an 1-inch band along all 4 edges of the filo.

Form a rectangular packet by folding the bottom edge of the filo up over the filling. Fold the right and left sides in about 1 1/2 inches as if you were making an envelope. If necessary, dab egg white on the upper corners. Fold down the top edge of the filo as if closing the flap of an envelope, and press gently to seal. Repeat with the remaining ingredients, working as quickly as possible.

Pour oil in a large shallow pan to a depth of about 1 inch and heat it until it reaches about 360°F or until a small piece of filo bubbles immediately when dipped into the oil. Slide the briks, one at a time, into the hot oil. Fry each brik for about 1 minute, or until the pastry puffs up and the bottom is golden brown. Using 2 spatulas, carefully turn the brik over and cook until the other side is golden brown and the egg is softly cooked, about 1 minute longer. Remove the briks to absorbent paper towels and drain them well. Serve immediately.

Briks or breks have long been a favorite Tunisian snack. These deep-fried pastry turnovers are made with dozens of different fillings stuffed into an unusual paper-thin dough that's similar to filo. So instead of tediously kneading semolina flour and water together to form the elastic malsouqua dough and then forming the pastry by dabbing the mass in concentric circles on a hot pan until you can peel off the pastry leaves, we use prepared filo. Thin spring roll wrappers are also an adequate substitute.

Note Because filo is very thin, you may want to use 2 sheets for each brik. Also, it's important to fry the briks soon after wrapping so that the pastry doesn't get soggy.

Fresh Figs Wrapped in Cinnamon-Scented Filo

Here, leaves of crisp, buttery filo pastry scented with cinnamon enclose warm figs and soft white chocolate. What a sensual dessert! Dust it with cinnamon and powdered sugar and serve warm with Raspberry Coulis (strained puréed raspberries moistened with a dash of cassis), warmed honey, or framboise (raspberry eau-de-vie) and whipped cream. When fresh figs are not in season, try substituting ripe peaches, apricots, or plums.

1/4 cup (1/2 stick) butter

1 teaspoon ground cinnamon

4 large ripe figs, preferably Black Mission

4 small squares white chocolate
(about 1/2 ounce each)

2 sheets filo

1/4 cup sugar

Cinnamon and confectioners' sugar,
for garnish

Preheat the oven to 375°F. In a small saucepan, melt the butter. Stir in the cinnamon and set the saucepan aside to cool. Trim the stems from the figs and cut a narrow slit in the stem end, stopping halfway down the length of the fig. Place a chocolate square in each fig and gently press the fig to close.

Cut the sheets of filo into 4-inch squares. You'll need 16 squares in all. Any leftover filo can be used in another recipe. Working with 4 squares of filo at a time, lightly brush one square with cinnamon butter and sprinkle it with sugar. Place the second square on top of the first, slightly askew, so the points of each square show. Butter and sugar the second square. Continue until all 4 squares are buttered, sugared, and placed on top of each other.

Place a fig in the center of the filo and carefully wrap the dough around the fig, twisting so it fits the fig snugly. Gently twist the filo just above the fig so there is a tuft of filo points sticking up on top like a piece of wrapped candy. Place the wrapped fig on a baking sheet. Repeat with the remaining figs and filo. Brush the tops with butter, then bake the wrapped figs until the filo is golden brown and the figs are heated through, 10 to 15 minutes. Serve warm, sprinkled with cinnamon and sugar.

Variation Baked Peaches Wrapped in Filo: Preheat the oven to 350°F. Substitute small ripe peaches for the figs. Split the peaches in half, remove the pits, then brush them with the cinnamon butter and sugar. Place the peaches on a baking sheet covered with parchment paper and bake them until softened, 15 to 20 minutes. Remove them from the oven and place a nugget of marzipan about the size of the peach pit in the center of each peach. Then wrap the peaches, cut side down, in the filo as described above. (Depending on the size of the peaches, you may need to use slightly larger squares of pastry.) Brush the tops with butter, then bake until the filo is crisp and golden brown, 12 to 15 minutes. Serve warm with plain or framboise-flavored whipped cream.

Ruby Poached Pears in Filo Nests with Chocolate Sauce

One 750-milliliter bottle red table wine

2 cups water

2 cups sugar

2 whole cloves

1 cinnamon stick

Grated zest of 1 lemon

Grated zest of 1 orange

10 small pears, no larger than 3 inches in diameter, preferably Seckel or French butter varieties, peeled (leave stems intact)

FILLING

2 tablespoons granulated sugar

2 tablespoons firmly packed brown sugar

1 teaspoon ground cinnamon

1 tablespoon butter

1/2 cup currants or other chopped dried fruit, softened in hot water and drained

FILO NESTS

6 to 8 sheets filo, depending on size of pears

About 1/4 cup (1/2 stick) butter, melted

1/4 cup sugar

1/4 cup finely chopped toasted pecans

Bittersweet Chocolate Sauce (recipe follows)

Makes 10 servings

Create a stunning presentation for this delicious dessert by arranging the filo-wrapped pears on serving plates whimsically garnished with chocolate sauce, raspberries, or fresh fig halves. Tuck a perky mint leaf near the stem of each pear before serving.

Feel free to use larger pears if you like. Simply cut the filo squares twice as large as the dimension of the pear at the widest part.

Poach the pears: In a large nonreactive saucepan, combine the wine, water, sugar, cloves, cinnamon stick, and lemon and orange zests. Bring the liquid to a boil. Add the pears, reduce the heat, and simmer for 20 to 30 minutes, until the pears are tender and a small knife inserted in the thickest part of a pear meets no resistance. Remove the pears with a slotted spoon and set them aside. Continue simmering the poaching liquid over high heat until it is reduced by half, about 20 minutes longer. Remove the saucepan from the heat and let the liquid cool. Return the pears to the liquid and refrigerate the mixture until ready to bake.

Prepare the filling: In a small bowl, combine the granulated sugar, brown sugar, and cinnamon. Cut in the butter with a pastry blender or fork until the mixture is crumbly. Then stir in the chopped currants. Remove the pears from the poaching liquid and, using a small melon baller, core them from the bottom, leaving the stem intact. Stuff the pears with 1 to 1 1/2 teaspoons of the filling.

Preheat the oven to 350°F. Cut each sheet of filo in half along the shorter side and into thirds along the longer side, to make six 6-inch squares per sheet. Working with 4 squares of filo at a time, lightly brush each with melted butter, then top with a sprinkle of sugar and nuts. Stack the 4 squares on top of one another. Place a pear in the center of the stacked filo squares and gather the filo up so that it encloses the pear. Twist the corners of the filo around the stem of the pear. Then brush the outside of the pastry with additional melted butter. Repeat with the remaining filo squares and pears.

Place the wrapped pears on parchment-lined baking sheets and bake them for 12 to 15 minutes, until the pastry is golden brown and the pears are warmed through. Serve warm with chocolate sauce.

Bittersweet Chocolate Sauce

Makes about 1 1/2 cups

10 ounces bittersweet chocolate, finely
   chopped

1 teaspoon vanilla extract

1/2 cup milk, or more if a thinner sauce
   is desired

In a bain-marie or in the top of a double boiler over gently simmering water, combine the chocolate and milk. Cook, stirring, until the chocolate melts and the mixture is smooth. Remove the sauce from the heat and stir in the vanilla. Serve warm.

Apple Streusel Strudel

APPLE FILLING

2 pounds tart apples (McIntosh,
    Gravenstein, Granny Smith), peeled,
    cored, and cut into 1/4-inch cubes

1 cup sugar

3 tablespoons cornstarch

1 tablespoon lemon juice

1 teaspoon ground cinnamon

Pinch of ground nutmeg

STREUSEL

1 cup all-purpose flour

1/2 cup firmly packed brown sugar

1/2 cup (1 stick) butter, cut into 1/2-inch
    pieces

1/4 cup regular rolled oats

1/2 teaspoon ground cinnamon

FILO WRAPPER

1/4 cup sugar

2 tablespoons finely chopped pecans

12 sheets filo

1/2 cup (1 stick) butter, melted

Makes 12 servings

A crunchy streusel topping sets these apple strudels apart from others that you may have had. They are simple to make and always popular.

Prepare the filling: Place the apples, sugar, cornstarch, lemon juice, cinnamon, and nutmeg in a saucepan. Cook the mixture over medium heat, stirring occasionally, until it thickens and the apples soften but still have some texture, about 10 minutes.

Prepare the streusel: In a bowl, blend together the flour, brown sugar, butter pieces, oats, and cinnamon with a pastry blender or fork until the mixture is crumbly. Set aside.

Preheat the oven to 350°F. Combine the sugar and pecans in a small bowl. Lay a sheet of filo on a flat work surface with the long side parallel to the edge of the surface. Brush the sheet of filo with melted butter and lightly sprinkle with some of the sugar and pecans. Top with another sheet of filo. Repeat brushing the filo with melted butter and sprinkling with a small amount of the sugar and pecans until you have stacked 6 sheets of filo on top of one other.

Spoon half of the apple filling in a line along the long edge about 1 inch from the bottom of the filo and 2 inches from the short sides. Fold the right and left sides of the filo about 2 inches over the apple filling, then roll it up from the bottom like a jelly roll. Transfer the strudel to a parchment-lined baking sheet. Proceed to make the second strudel and place it on the baking sheet next to the first one. Brush the tops of both strudels with melted butter and sprinkle with the streusel. Bake for 12 to 15 minutes until golden brown. Serve hot or at room temperature.

Chicken Roulade with Prosciutto,
Spinach, and Pine Nuts

Leeks Wrapped in Prosciutto
with Sauce Verte

Grilled Radicchio Wrapped
in Pancetta

Balsamic Vinaigrette

Braciole di Tonno Fresco
(Grilled Tuna Rolls)

Salmoriglio Sauce

Meat, Chicken, and Smoked Fish

You could say that in the classic dish Chicken Kiev, boneless chicken breasts become a "wrap" for a chunk of herbed butter. Lightly pounded boneless, skinless chicken, in fact, is a versatile wrap. A recipe for Chicken Roulade follows that features chicken enclosing a tasty filling of prosciutto, spinach, and pine nuts. You could also stuff chicken with fresh goat cheese, roasted red peppers, and strips of fresh basil. Or try a variety of sautéed diced vegetables mixed with risotto. There are endless variations.

Prosciutto is another terrific wrap. Wind it around blanched young asparagus or braised leeks, wedges of grilled red chard or radicchio, caramelized pears or strawberries sprinkled with balsamic vinegar. Or substitute thinly sliced Black Forest or Westphalian ham for the prosciutto. Children love thinly sliced cured ham wrapped around fat pretzels.

Smoked salmon is another natural wrap. Spread thin slices with chive cream cheese and wrap around baby artichoke hearts, asparagus spears, thin seedless cucumber sticks, or small pieces of braised fennel.

In Braciole di Tonno Fresco, thinly sliced tuna fillets are rolled around a savory bread stuffing and lightly grilled. These are just a few ideas for hearty meat, poultry, and seafood wraps.

Chicken Roulade with Prosciutto, Spinach, and Pine Nuts

Makes 4 servings

Thin chicken breast fillets become a delicious and versatile wrap for a variety of vegetables, including sweet peppers, zucchini ribbons, and sautéed mushrooms, as well as cheese. Chèvre or domestic goat cheese and fontina work especially well baked inside chicken. Serve this attractive dish as an entrée or slice it and serve on small pieces of toasted baguette as an hors d'oeuvre.

4 boneless, skinless chicken breast halves (about 5 ounces each)
2 1/2 tablespoons extra virgin olive oil
About 3 1/2 cups loosely packed fresh spinach, washed and stems removed
Salt to taste
Freshly ground black pepper to taste
Pinch of ground nutmeg
1/4 cup pine nuts, toasted
3 cloves garlic, finely minced
1 lemon, cut in half
4 paper-thin slices prosciutto
4 thin slices pancetta or bacon
4 sprigs rosemary
Lemon wedges for garnish (optional)

Remove the small tenderloin from the undersides of the chicken breasts and save them for another use. Place the chicken breasts, smooth side up, between 2 pieces of plastic wrap and pound to 1/4-inch thickness.

Heat 2 tablespoons of the oil in a large frying pan over medium heat. Add the spinach, stirring so that the spinach wilts evenly and the water evaporates. Season with 1/2 teaspoon salt, 1/4 teaspoon pepper, and nutmeg. When the spinach is wilted and nearly dry, 3 to 5 minutes, add the pine nuts and garlic, cooking just until the garlic is fragrant, about 30 seconds. Squeeze the juice from one lemon half over the spinach. Remove the pan from the heat and let it cool briefly.

Preheat the oven to 350°F. On a clean work surface, lay a chicken breast down on what would have been the skin side. Top it with a slice of prosciutto that is slightly smaller than the piece of chicken. Top with a thin layer of spinach. Starting at the pointed end, roll the breast up. Wrap the middle of the rolled chicken breast with a slice of pancetta or bacon. Tuck a sprig of rosemary under the pancetta. Secure the wrapped roll with a toothpick. Repeat with the remaining chicken breasts. Brush them with the remaining olive oil, season lightly with salt and pepper, and sprinkle with the juice from the remaining lemon half.

Bake the chicken, basting occasionally with pan juices, for about 15 minutes, until the internal temperature of the chicken reaches 160°F on a meat thermometer. Do not overcook. If the chicken is done but the bacon isn't crisp, place the rolled breasts under the broiler for a minute.

To serve, cut the rolls in half diagonally. Pour any pan juices over the chicken and serve with lemon wedges, if desired.

Prosciutto

Prosciutto wrapped around melon is a classic first course in northern Italy. Prosciutto, an intensely flavored salt-cured dried ham, is also delicious wrapped around ripe figs, fresh or caramelized pears, or strawberries sprinkled with balsamic vinegar. There are also many delicious combinations of prosciutto and vegetables, like prosciutto-wrapped blanched asparagus spears served with a delicate orange mint mayonnaise. Another favorite prosciutto and vegetable recipe follows.

Leeks Wrapped in Prosciutto with Sauce Verte

Makes 8 servings

Leeks have so much wonderful flavor, it's a good idea to save the cooking liquid for using in soups, cooking risotto, or making other recipes. If you can't find young leeks, use slightly larger ones and allow one leek per serving. Just increase the braising time.

Sauce verte is a classic French sauce with a fresh herbal flavor that's delicious spooned over grilled fish or chicken. You can vary the recipe by adding chives, basil, chervil, or nearly any other herb.

16 small leeks, less than $3/4$ inch in diameter

1 quart homemade or low-sodium canned chicken stock

2 shallots, peeled

$1/2$ cup fresh parsley leaves

1 tablespoon chopped fresh tarragon or 1 teaspoon leaves from tarragon vinegar

1 cup mayonnaise

Few drops Worcestershire sauce

16 slices prosciutto

Trim the leeks by cutting off the root end, being careful to leave the leaves attached. Remove any wilted leaves and cut the tops off about 2 inches from the point at which the white becomes green. Slit each leek from the leaf end down to where the white begins. Rinse well under running cold water to remove any sand.

Place the leeks in a single layer in a large frying pan. Pour in enough chicken stock to nearly cover the leeks and bring the stock to a boil. Cover the pan, reduce the heat to a simmer, and cook until the leeks are tender, about 15 minutes. Remove the pan from the heat. Remove the leeks from the pan with a slotted spoon and let them cool. Reserve the stock to use in other recipes.

Prepare the sauce verte: Drop the shallots through the feed tube of a food processor or blender while it is running. Add the parsley and tarragon leaves and pulse several times. Then add the mayonnaise and Worcestershire sauce and continue processing until the sauce is smooth. If you don't have a food processor, finely mince the shallots, parsley, and tarragon. Then stir in the mayonnaise and Worcestershire sauce.

When the leeks are cool, wrap each one with a slice of prosciutto. Arrange the leeks on plates, allowing 2 leeks per serving. Top with a spoonful of sauce verte and serve the remaining sauce on the side.

Grilled Radicchio Wrapped in Pancetta

2 large heads radicchio, quartered
Extra virgin olive oil
8 slices (1/8 inch thick) pancetta or smoked bacon

Salt to taste
Freshly ground black pepper to taste

Quarter the heads of radicchio, removing any wilted outer leaves. Cut away most of the core, leaving just enough to hold the leaves together.

Brush the radicchio with the olive oil. Wrap 1 slice of pancetta or bacon around each quarter of radicchio, leaving about an inch of radicchio at both ends exposed. If necessary, secure the pancetta or bacon slice with a toothpick. Season with salt and pepper.

Preheat a broiler or gas grill to medium-low, or prepare a charcoal fire, allowing the coals to burn until they are evenly covered with a gray ash. Grill or broil the wrapped radicchio, turning once, until the pancetta is crisp and the radicchio begins to wilt. Take care not to char the radicchio too much. Serve warm, drizzled with Balsamic Vinaigrette.

Balsamic Vinaigrette

Makes about 3/4 cup

1/2 cup extra virgin olive oil
1/4 cup balsamic vinegar
3 shallots, minced (about 2 tablespoons)
Salt to taste
Freshly ground black pepper to taste

In a small bowl, mix the oil, vinegar, and shallots until well blended. Season with salt and pepper. Drizzle over the Grilled Radicchio.

Too bad that the pretty burgundy-colored leaves of radicchio are usually relegated to the salad bowl. They're delicious grilled, baked, or sautéed. In this delicious appetizer, the slightly bitter Italian chicory is wrapped with thin slices of pancetta (cured fresh Italian bacon) and then grilled over hot coals until the bacon is crisp and smoky flavored. Serve the wrapped leaves lightly drizzled with balsamic vinaigrette.

Braciole di Tonno Fresco
(Grilled Tuna Rolls)

Makes 8 servings

In this classic southern Italian recipe, thinly sliced fresh tuna becomes the wrap enclosing a savory mixture of garlicky bread crumbs, currants, capers, and sharp Pecorino cheese. It's a wonderful dish as part of a buffet or as a first course.

To ensure getting the freshest fish, always buy from a fishmonger you trust. For this recipe, ask the fishmonger to slice the tuna into $1/4$-inch-thick fillets. To do this at home, use a sharp slicing knife with the blade parallel to the cutting surface and cut the fish fillets in half horizontally.

Serve warm with Salmoriglio Sauce, a tangy lemon herb sauce (recipe follows).

8 tuna fillets ($1/4$ inch thick), each measuring approximately 4 inches square (about 2 pounds total)

FILLING
2 teaspoons olive oil
1 small yellow onion, finely diced
4 ounces tuna fillet, finely chopped
$1/3$ cup fresh bread crumbs
3 cloves garlic, minced
3 tablespoons chopped fresh parsley

$1/4$ cup (2 ounces) grated Pecorino cheese
1 extra-large egg
2 tablespoons dried currants, softened in hot water and drained
1 tablespoon capers, rinsed and chopped
$1/4$ teaspoon salt, or to taste
Freshly ground black pepper to taste

FINISHING
3 tablespoons olive oil
$1/4$ cup fresh bread crumbs

Place each slice of tuna between 2 pieces of parchment and lightly pound it with a mallet to flatten the fish slightly, taking care not to break it up. Refrigerate the tuna while preparing the filling.

Prepare the filling: Heat the oil in a small frying pan over medium heat. Add the onion and sauté for 2 minutes, or until the onion has softened. Add the chopped fish, bread crumbs, garlic, and parsley and cook 3 minutes more, until the onion is translucent. Remove the pan from the heat and let it cool. Stir in the cheese, egg, currants, and capers. Season with salt and pepper.

Remove each piece of tuna from its parchment paper layers. Smear about 1 tablespoon of the filling on each piece. Roll up the tuna slices, pushing any excess filling inside. Secure each tuna roll with a toothpick. Brush the tuna rolls with 2 tablespoons of the olive oil and dredge in the bread crumbs, pressing the bread crumbs on firmly with your fingers.

In a large, preferably nonstick frying pan, heat the remaining 1 tablespoon olive oil over medium-high heat. Sauté the tuna rolls, half at a time, for about 2 minutes per side. (You can also broil the tuna rolls about 6 inches from the source of heat for about 3 minutes per side.) Remove the toothpicks. Serve immediately with Salmoriglio Sauce.

Salmoriglio Sauce

Makes about 1 cup

1/2 cup olive oil
Juice of 2 lemons
2 tablespoons hot water
1 tablespoon chopped fresh parsley
1 tablespoon chopped fresh oregano

Place the oil in a medium bowl. Whisking constantly, slowly add the lemon juice, then the water, until the mixture thickens and becomes frothy. Whisk in the parsley and oregano. Serve immediately or keep warm in a bain-marie or top of a double boiler over, but not in, simmering water.

It's best to prepare this sauce ahead and keep it warm. The tuna is done in a flash, and you don't want to risk over-cooking the fish while you make the sauce.

Empanada Dough

Artichoke and Fennel Empanadas

Caramelized Onion and Smoked Trout
Empanadas

Jamaican Shrimp Patties

Wet Jerk Marinade

Beef Empanadillas

English Savory Fruit Pasties

Chef Jeanne's All-Purpose Pie Dough

Bourbon Pecan Mini-Pies

Mini Blackberry Hand Pies

Samosas

Spicy Fruit Turnovers

Triple-Chocolate Pasticiotti
with Hazelnut Crust

Pastry

Small pies, patties, and turnovers are featured in many of the world's cuisines, but it's doubtful that any cultures are more passionate about them than the people of Central and South America, who snack on them from dawn to dusk. Cooks in Latin countries bake a stunning variety of individual pies in various sizes and shapes. Savory three-bite pastries are called *empanadas,* while smaller, one-bite versions are referred to as *empanaditas* or *empanadillas.* Innovative bakers stuff these flaky pastries with nearly any savory mixture you can imagine, including duck, quail, pork, venison, pheasant, lamb, goat, rabbit, and fresh and smoked fish.

The main consideration in creating such a wrap is to season the filling boldly enough to stand up to rich doughs like the one for our empanadas. In this chapter you'll find filling recipes based on artichokes and fresh fennel, jerked shrimp, and caramelized onions with smoked trout. There's also a recipe for tantalizing beef empanadillas featuring a spicy beef, olive, and raisin mixture stuffed into tiny rounds of cumin-scented cream cheese dough. In addition, there's also a recipe for traditional Cornish pasties, as well as one for samosas that will please everyone who craves Indian food.

This chapter also includes a wonderful basic pie dough recipe with variations for making miniature blackberry pies, Bourbon Pecan Mini-Pies, and a spicy fruit turnover filling. Finally, there is a triple-chocolate pastry with a hazelnut crust enclosing a decadent chocolate cream filling.

A note about storage: Empanadas and other small filled pastries are best eaten warm, while the pastry is still crisp, or at room temperature. If the filling is very dry and doesn't contain perishable meat or seafood, you can store them at room temperature in an airtight container. However, pastries filled with perishable mixtures, especially those containing cream or eggs, should be refrigerated or frozen. To recrisp the pastry, place the pies in a 350°F oven for about 5 minutes. For longer storage, pastry chefs recommend freezing the pastries in an airtight container.

Empanada Dough

5 cups all-purpose flour
1 1/2 teaspoons salt
1/2 teaspoon baking powder
1 1/4 cups (2 1/2 sticks) cold butter,
    cut into 1-inch pieces

4 extra-large eggs
1/3 cup milk

Makes 36 empanadas

This basic dough works beautifully for both savory and sweet pastries. The addition of the eggs gives a lovely yellow color to the pastry when it's baked. An added bonus is that it doesn't shrink as much as pie dough. It's important, however, to make sure the dough is well chilled and not to overwork it.

Note To use the scraps of dough, layer the pieces, then reroll, cutting out more rounds.

In a large bowl, combine the flour, salt, and baking powder. Using a pastry cutter or 2 knives, cut in the butter until the mixture is crumbly. In a small bowl, beat 3 of the eggs and the milk together. Add the egg and milk mixture to the flour mixture all at once and stir gently just until it holds together, forming a smooth, soft dough. Divide the dough in half and wrap each portion tightly in plastic wrap, gently pressing each portion into a disk. Refrigerate the disks for at least 2 hours to let the dough rest.

With your filling ready, preheat the oven to 375°F and remove 1 disk of dough from the refrigerator. On a lightly floured board, roll out the dough to a thickness of 1/8 inch. Using a 4-inch biscuit cutter, cut the dough into rounds.

Place 1 tablespoon of filling on half of each round. Moisten the edges of the rounds with water. Fold the pastry over the filling, forming a half-moon, and press the edges together. Crimp the edges with the tines of a fork. Place the filled pastries on baking sheets. Lightly beat the remaining egg and brush the egg on top of each pastry. Bake for 16 to 18 minutes, until the pastry is golden brown. Repeat with the remaining half of the dough.

Artichoke and Fennel Empanadas

Makes 36 empanadas

These savory empanadas
have a decidedly Spanish
flavor. Serve them for tapas.

1 tablespoon butter

1 yellow onion, thinly sliced

1 leek, white part only, cut in half
   lengthwise, rinsed, and thinly sliced

1 small fennel bulb (about 1/2 pound)

4 cloves garlic, minced

3 tablespoons dry sherry

2 jars (6 ounces each) marinated artichoke
   hearts, rinsed, drained well, and
   coarsely chopped

2 tablespoons chopped fresh parsley

1/2 teaspoon salt

1/4 teaspoon freshly ground black pepper

1 recipe Empanada Dough (page 103)

Melt the butter in a large frying pan over medium heat. Add the onion and leek and cook, stirring, until softened, about 10 minutes.

Trim off the leaves from the fennel and any tough outer parts. Cut the fennel bulb into quarters lengthwise. Cut a thin slice from the bottom of each quarter and remove and discard the core. Then cut each quarter across into thin slices. Add the fennel to the frying pan, reduce the heat to low, and simmer for 15 minutes, stirring occasionally, until the vegetables are tender.

Add the garlic and sherry and cook 1 minute longer. Add the artichokes, parsley, salt, and pepper. Mix thoroughly, then remove the pan from the heat and let cool.

Follow the directions on page 103 for filling and cooking the empanadas.

Caramelized Onion and
Smoked Trout Empanadas

1 tablespoon butter

4 medium onions, cut in half and
    thinly sliced

1 medium-large (about 8 ounces) russet
    potato, peeled and cut into 1/4-inch
    cubes

1 boneless smoked trout (about 5 ounces)

2 tablespoons minced fresh chives

1 teaspoon chopped fresh thyme

1/4 teaspoon freshly ground black pepper

1 recipe Empanada Dough (page 103)

Makes 36 empanadas

Bake this fabulous mixture inside flaky pastry or use as a filling for filo triangles or omelets. The only time-consuming part is cooking the onions down until they become jamlike and turn nearly as dark as mahogany. You may want to caramelize several pounds of onions in advance and keep them in the refrigerator to use in this and other recipes.

Melt the butter in a large frying pan over medium-high heat. Add the onions and cook, stirring constantly, for about 5 minutes, until they begin to wilt. Reduce the heat to low and cook, stirring occasionally, until the onions are soft and deep golden brown. This may take an hour, depending on the temperature and the amount of onions you're caramelizing, but you need to pay close attention only during the final 10 minutes or so to prevent burning. Remove the onions to a bowl.

While the onions are cooking, bring a large pot of water to a boil. Salt generously, add the potato, and cook until it is tender, about 5 minutes. Drain the potato and place in the bowl with the onions.

Remove the skin from the trout. Flake the flesh of the fish into the bowl with the other ingredients, being careful to discard any bones you may find. Gently stir in the chives, thyme, and pepper.

Follow the directions on page 103 for filling and cooking the empanadas.

Jamaican Shrimp Patties

Makes 36 empanadas

Jamaica is known for jerk seasoning, a mixture of spices—usually chiles, thyme, cinnamon, allspice, and cloves—garlic, and onion that is used as a rub for pork, chicken, and other meats. Today you can buy various forms of prepared jerk seasoning rather than making it yourself. In this recipe, a liquid jerk marinade spices up sweet shrimp and pine-apple. The filling is delicious baked in empanada dough or other flaky pastry.

1 pound bay shrimp (about 2 cups)
1 can (8 ounces) crushed pineapple, well drained
1/3 cup finely chopped red onion
2 tablespoons chopped fresh cilantro
2 cloves garlic, minced
1 tablespoon grated fresh ginger
1 tablespoon Wet Jerk Marinade (recipe follows) or 1 to 2 tablespoons commercial jerk marinade
1/2 teaspoon salt
1 recipe Empanada Dough (page 103)

In a large bowl, combine the shrimp, pineapple, onion, cilantro, garlic, ginger, jerk marinade, and salt. Stir to blend the mixture well.

Follow the directions on page 103 for filling and cooking the empanadas.

Wet Jerk Marinade

1 small sweet onion, finely chopped

1/4 cup ground allspice

3 habanero or Scotch bonnet chiles,
    seeded and finely chopped

Grated zest and juice of 2 limes
    (about 1/4 cup juice)

Grated zest and juice of 1 orange

1 tablespoon ground cinnamon

1 tablespoon ground nutmeg

2 tablespoons cider vinegar

1 tablespoon molasses

2 teaspoons salt

In a blender, combine all of the ingredients and process until the mixture is fairly smooth, scraping down the sides of the blender jar as needed. Store in the refrigerator. Let the marinade stand for about a day before using to allow the flavors to blend.

Makes about 1 1/4 cups

Traditionally, the ingredients for this spicy jerk seasoning are pounded together in a mortar and pestle. To save time, you can use a blender or small food processor. This fiery seasoning mixture will keep several months stored in a tightly covered clean jar in the refrigerator.

Beef Empanadillas

Makes about 30 empanadillas

South Americans are passionate about empanadas. Traditionally, the dough for these small pastry turnovers is made with flour, lard, eggs, and water. This recipe takes a delicious break from authenticity; the easy-to-make cream cheese and cornmeal dough is scented with nutty-flavored ground cumin and a pinch of cayenne.

The well-seasoned filling combines ground beef with sweet raisins, piquant olives, and colorful bits of pimiento. Don't limit yourself to beef. Ground turkey, coarsely chopped pork, chicken, or even lamb works beautifully.

SPICY BEEF FILLING

2 tablespoons olive oil

1 small onion, cut in half and thinly sliced

3 cloves garlic, minced

1/2 pound ground beef

3 tablespoons dry sherry or dry white wine

1/4 cup golden raisins

1/4 cup Kalamata olives, pitted and thinly sliced

1/4 cup diced pimiento

1 tablespoon minced fresh oregano or 1 1/2 teaspoons dried

1/2 teaspoon salt

1/4 teaspoon cayenne pepper

1/4 teaspoon freshly ground black pepper

CUMIN-FLAVORED EMPANADA DOUGH

1/2 cup (1 stick) unsalted butter, at room temperature

4 ounces cream cheese, at room temperature

1 1/2 cups all-purpose flour

1/4 cup cornmeal

1 teaspoon ground cumin

Pinch of salt

Pinch of cayenne pepper

1 egg

1 tablespoon water

Prepare the filling: Heat the oil in a large frying pan over medium-high heat. Add the onion and sauté until it is translucent, about 4 minutes. Stir in the garlic and cook 1 minute more. Add the beef and cook, stirring, until the meat is browned, about 5 minutes. Drain off any excess fat. Add the sherry, raisins, olives, pimiento, oregano, salt, cayenne, and black pepper and cook over medium-low heat about 10 minutes longer to meld the flavors. Remove the pan from the heat and allow to cool.

Prepare the pastry: In the bowl of a food processor, combine all the ingredients except the egg and water, pulsing several times. Process 1 to 2 minutes, until the dough forms a ball; do not overwork the dough. If you don't have a food processor, beat the butter and cream cheese until smooth. Then stir in the flour, cornmeal, cumin, salt and cayenne to form a soft dough.

Remove the dough from the bowl, wrap it tightly in plastic, and refrigerate it for 30 minutes to let it rest. Preheat the oven to 400°F.

On a floured surface, roll out the dough to a thickness of 1/8 inch. With a 3-inch round cutter, cut out rounds of dough. Place about 1 1/2 teaspoons of filling in the middle of each round. In a small bowl, thoroughly combine the egg and water. Brush the egg wash on the inside edges of the dough. Fold the dough in half, enclosing the filling. Crimp the edges with a fork.

Place the empanadillas on baking sheets and brush the tops with the egg wash. Bake them for about 15 minutes, until the pastry is golden brown.

English Savory Fruit Pasties

SAVORY MEAT FILLING

2 cups beef stock

1 large carrot, cut into $^1/4$-inch cubes

1 medium russet potato, peeled and cut into $^1/4$-inch cubes

1 small turnip, cut into $^1/4$-inch cubes

1 small onion, diced

$^1/2$ pound cooked beef, cut into $^1/4$-inch cubes (about 1 cup)

1 teaspoon chopped fresh thyme

1 teaspoon Worcestershire sauce

Salt to taste

Freshly ground white pepper to taste

APPLE FILLING

1 tablespoon butter

1 large tart cooking apple, preferably Pippin or Granny Smith, peeled, cored, and cut into $^1/4$-inch cubes

$^1/4$ cup sugar

$^1/4$ teaspoon ground cloves

PASTRY

$1^1/2$ cups all-purpose flour

Pinch of salt

$^3/4$ cup shortening

4 tablespoons cold water

1 egg, beaten

Makes 6 pasties

Pasties, savory meat and potato mixtures baked inside flaky pastry, were developed in mid-eighteenth-century England as "to-go" food for miners to tote to work. Chef Kevin Duffy remembers his mother separating fruit and meat fillings in the same hand pie for his father, who worked long shifts down in the coal mines of northern England. Traditionally, says Duffy, the fillings were cooked in the pastry, but he prefers to cook the filling ahead of time, reducing the final baking time and producing a moister pasty.

You can substitute cooked chicken, turkey, or pork for the beef, and chicken stock for the beef stock.

Prepare the savory meat filling: Bring the stock to a boil in a stainless steel or other nonreactive saucepan. Add the vegetables and cook until the mixture returns to a boil. Lift out the vegetables, reserving the stock. Allow the vegetables and the stock to cool.

In a mixing bowl, gently combine the vegetables with the beef, thyme, and Worcestershire sauce. Moisten the mixture with 2 to 3 tablespoons of the reserved stock. Taste for seasoning and add salt and pepper, if necessary. Save the reserved stock for other recipes. Refrigerate the filling until ready to assemble the pasties.

Prepare the apple filling: Heat the butter in a frying pan over low heat. Mix in the apple, sugar, and cloves. Cook, stirring occasionally, until the apple is tender but not mushy, about 5 minutes. Remove from the heat and set aside to cool.

Make the pastry: Combine the flour and salt in a mixing bowl. Cut in the shortening with a pastry blender or 2 knives until the mixture is crumbly. Add the water, little by little, until the dough holds together and comes away from the sides of the bowl. If you are using only the meat filling, you may want to season the dough with your choice of dill, dried thyme, ground cumin, or a few threads of saffron dissolved in water. Wrap the dough in plastic and chill for about 30 minutes.

To assemble: Roll out the dough on a lightly floured work surface to a thickness of $1/8$ inch. Using a 6-inch-diameter saucer or bowl or a round cutter, cut the dough into 6 rounds. Save the trimmings.

Divide the meat filling into 6 portions. Place 1 portion of the filling on $2/3$ of a pastry round, leaving a $1/2$-inch border of dough along the outer edge. Repeat, dividing the meat among the other pastry rounds. Roll out the reserved pastry trimmings into a 6-inch square and cut it into 6 strips. Lay a strip of pastry against the meat filling in each pastry round, trimming the ends of the strip flush with the pastry round. Divide the apple filling into 6 portions. Place 1 portion (about $1/4$ cup) of the filling on the remaining $1/3$ of each pastry round, leaving a $1/4$-inch border.

Preheat the oven to 375°F. Brush the edges of the pastry rounds with beaten egg. Hold a pastry in the palm of one hand and use the other hand to bring the 2 sides of the pastry up over the fillings, being careful to prevent them from oozing out. The pastry will look like a half-moon-shaped turnover with the meat and fruit fillings separated by a layer of pastry inside. Press the edges together to seal. Crimp the edges with a fork, if desired. Place the filled pasties on a parchment-lined baking sheet. Cut a small slit in the top of each pastry to allow steam to escape. Brush the top of each pastry with beaten egg.

Bake the pasties for 15 to 18 minutes, until they are golden brown. Remove them from the oven and allow to cool slightly before serving, or chill them and serve later.

Chef Jeanne's All-Purpose Pie Dough

2 cups all-purpose flour
3/4 cup (1 1/2 sticks) cold unsalted butter,
*   cut into 1-inch cubes*

1 teaspoon sugar
1/2 teaspoon salt
1/3 cup ice-cold water

In a large bowl, stir together the flour, butter, and sugar. Using a pastry cutter or 2 knives, cut in the butter until the pieces are pea-sized.

Dissolve the salt in the water. Add the water, mixing only until the dough forms a ball. Wrap the ball of dough tightly in plastic and flatten it slightly. Refrigerate the dough for about 1 hour.

On a lightly floured board, roll out the dough to a thickness of 1/8 inch.

To make raviolini, cut the dough into 2 1/2-inch squares, fill them, and fold them in half. To make mini turnovers, cut the dough into 2 1/2-inch squares, fill them, and fold them over to form triangles. To make mini beggar's purses, cut the dough into 3-inch rounds, fill them, then gather the dough up to meet in the center, forming a bundle, and pinch to seal. To make mini-crostades, cut the dough in 4-inch rounds, fill them, and bring the edges almost together (allow some filling to be exposed).

Bake the pastries in a 350°F oven for 10 to 12 minutes, until they are golden brown.

Use this dough for miniature turnovers, beggar's purses, tarts, or pies. Any extra pieces of dough make delicious cookies: brush the rolled-out dough lightly with softened butter, sprinkle with cinnamon and sugar, and bake the pastry until golden brown.

To produce flaky dough, make sure that the butter and water are cold, and don't overmix. It's also a good idea to dissolve the salt in the water to ensure that it's mixed in evenly.

Bourbon Pecan Mini-Pies

Makes 24 mini-pies

These delicious bite-size pies transport us to days of leisurely living and genteel hospitality. You can leave the bourbon out, if you want. The flavor will be different but still delectable. For variation, use toasted almonds instead of pecans and amaretto in place of the bourbon, or try toasted hazelnuts and Frangelico.

1 recipe Chef Jeanne's All-Purpose Pie Dough (page 111)
2 tablespoons (1 ounce) butter, melted
1/4 cup firmly packed brown sugar
1 extra-large egg
1 tablespoon bourbon
1/4 cup dark corn syrup
Pinch of salt
4 ounces pecan halves (heaping 1/2 cup)

On a lightly floured board, roll the dough out to a thickness of 1/8 inch. (Try to create a roughly rectangular or square shape as you do this.) Cut the rolled dough into twenty-four 2 1/2-inch squares. Tuck the squares of dough into mini-muffin pans (1 3/4 to 2 inches wide when measured at the top).

Preheat the oven to 400°F. In a mixing bowl, combine the butter and sugar. Beat in the egg and continue to beat until the mixture is fluffy. Stir in the bourbon, corn syrup, and salt. Place 3 to 4 pecan halves in the bottom of each pastry-lined muffin cup. Whisk the bourbon mixture, then spoon 1/2 table-spoon over the pecans for each mini-pie. Gently fold the corners of the pastry over the filling.

Bake the pies on the middle rack of the oven for 10 minutes. Reduce the oven temperature to 350°F and bake 12 to 15 minutes longer, until the pastry is golden brown.

Remove the muffin pans from the oven. Let stand until cool enough to handle. Pry out each miniature pie with the rounded tip of a dinner knife. Serve warm or at room temperature.

Mini Blackberry Hand Pies

2 cups fresh or thawed frozen
    blackberries
1/2 cup plus 2 tablespoons sugar
1 tablespoon cornstarch
1/2 tablespoon lemon juice
1 teaspoon ground cinnamon
1/2 teaspoon vanilla extract

1/4 teaspoon ground cloves
Pinch of ground cardamom
1 recipe Chef Jeanne's All-Purpose Pie
    Dough (page 111)
1/3 cup finely chopped walnuts
2 tablespoons very cold butter, cut into
    24 little cubes

Makes 24 hand pies

These bite-size blackberry pies have just a hint of cloves in the filling and are absolutely delicious.

Preheat the oven to 450°F. If you are using fresh berries, rinse and drain them. In a large bowl, combine the berries, 1/2 cup of the sugar, the cornstarch, lemon juice, cinnamon, vanilla, cloves, and cardamom. Stir gently just to combine the ingredients.

On a lightly floured surface, roll out the dough to a thickness of 1/8 inch. (Try to create a roughly rectangular or square shape as you do this.) Cut the rolled dough into twenty-four 2 1/2-inch squares. Tuck the squares of dough into mini-muffin pans (1 3/4 to 2 inches wide when measured at the top).

Place 1/4 teaspoon walnuts in each pastry-lined muffin cup. Place 1 heaping teaspoon of the filling on top of the walnuts. Dot with 1 cube of butter. Fold the pastry edges over the filling. Brush the tops of the hand pies with water and sprinkle the remaining 2 tablespoons sugar over all.

Place the muffin pans on the middle rack of the oven and bake for 8 minutes. Reduce the oven temperature to 350°F and bake an additional 10 minutes, until the pies are golden brown. Remove the pans from the oven and let stand until cool enough to handle. Use the rounded tip of a table knife to loosen the pies from the muffin cups. Remove to a rack and allow to cool slightly before serving, or serve at room temperature.

Samosas

Makes 24 samosas

If you wandered through an Indian bazaar, you might get the idea that snacking is the country's national pastime and that samosas are one of the most popular snacks. These triangular-shaped deep-fried pastries are usually filled with a spicy mélange of potatoes, sometimes combined with green peas or with a highly seasoned meat filling.

Several of the ingredients may not be familiar. Garam masala (a blend of aromatic roasted spices), intensely sour-flavored mango powder, and the exceptionally aromatic asafetida or heeng are all available at Indian markets and are becoming increasingly available at supermarkets. If you can't find mango powder,

DOUGH
3 cups all-purpose flour
1/4 cup shortening
1/2 teaspoon salt
3/4 cup cold water

POTATO FILLING
2 large russet potatoes
1/4 cup canola oil
2 tablespoons ground coriander
1 tablespoon garam masala

1 tablespoon mango powder
1 tablespoon finely minced
    fresh ginger
1/2 tablespoon ground cumin
1/4 teaspoon asafetida
1/4 teaspoon cayenne pepper
1/2 cup fresh or frozen peas
    (optional)
1 teaspoon salt, or to taste

Oil for deep-frying

Prepare the dough: Place the flour, shortening, and salt in a food processor and pulse several times, until mixture is crumbly. Add the water through the feed tube, continuing to process for about 1 minute, or until the dough comes together. Remove the dough to a lightly floured surface and knead it for about 30 seconds. Cover the dough with a damp kitchen towel and let it rest for about 30 minutes.

Prepare the filling: Place the unpeeled potatoes in a pot. Add enough boiling water to cover and cook until the potatoes are tender, 20 to 30 minutes. Drain. When cool enough to handle, peel and cut into 1/4-inch cubes.

In a large frying pan, heat the canola oil over medium-high heat. Add the coriander, garam masala, mango powder, ginger, cumin, asafetida, and cayenne. Cook, toasting the spices, for about 2 minutes, stirring continuously. Stir in the cooked potatoes, distributing the spices evenly throughout the potatoes. Toss in the peas, if desired, and season to taste with salt. Remove the pan from the heat and let it cool.

Make a thin paste by mixing about 1/4 cup flour and 1/3 cup water in a small bowl or cup. On a lightly floured board, roll the dough into a rope about 24 inches long. Cut the dough into 1-inch pieces and form each piece into a ball. Then flatten each ball into a 1 1/2-inch round.

Lightly reflour the board and roll out the rounds of dough into 10×7-inch ovals. Cut each oval horizontally in half. Brush a light film of the dissolved flour paste along half of the straight side. Holding the semicircle of dough in your hand with the rounded side on the top, form a cone by overlapping the moistened portion of pastry over the dry portion by about 1/8 inch, making sure that the point is closed. Press the edges securely to seal.

Spoon about 1 tablespoon of filling into the cone. Moisten the edge of the rounded side on top with the flour-water paste and bring it over the filling and pinch the pastry together to seal in the filling. Set aside while you form the remaining samosas.

Heat about 2 inches of oil in a deep heavy frying pan or deep-fryer to about 375°F (bubbles will immediately form when you dip an end of the samosa into the oil). Drop in about 6 samosas at a time and reduce the heat to about 300°F, a low simmer, so that the dough does not brown too quickly. Deep-fry the samosas, turning once, until they are golden brown, 12 to 15 minutes. Drain on paper towels. Fried samosas can be kept hot for about half an hour in a warm oven on a baking sheet lined with paper towels. Serve the samosas hot.

Note Samosas can also be frozen. Deep-fry the samosas in oil heated to about 350°F for about 2 minutes. (This step prevents the dough from becoming soggy.) Drain them on paper towels. Then pack them into freezer containers. To reheat, arrange the frozen samosas on baking sheets and place them on the center shelf of a preheated 350°F oven and bake for about 25 minutes.

substitute lemon juice. Wait to add it until after you remove the filling mixture from the heat. The flavor won't be quite as tart, but it is close.

When Chef Sukhi Singh, cooking teacher in the San Francisco Bay area, makes samosas by the hundreds, she saves time by using the thinnest possible flour tortillas. Traditionally, however, the dough is made by hand. This is her recipe.

Spicy Fruit Turnovers

Makes 36 turnovers

A spicy fruit filling makes
a delicious dessert turnover.

FILLING

1 cup diced dried apricots

1/2 cup coarsely chopped dark raisins

1/2 cup coarsely chopped golden raisins

2 cups boiling water

1 cup firmly packed brown sugar

1 cup heavy cream

1/2 cup chopped pecans, toasted

2 tablespoons diced candied orange peel

1/2 teaspoon ground cinnamon

1/2 teaspoon ground cloves

PIE DOUGH

4 cups all-purpose flour

1 1/2 cups (3 sticks) cold unsalted butter,
   cut into 1-inch cubes

2 teaspoons sugar

1 teaspoon salt

2/3 cup ice cold water

1 egg, slightly beaten

Prepare the filling: Combine the apricots and raisins in a large bowl. Pour the boiling water over the fruit and let stand for about 10 minutes to soften the fruit. Drain the mixture well, discarding the water.

In a small saucepan, combine the sugar and cream. Bring to a boil, stirring until the sugar is dissolved. Reduce the heat and simmer for 6 minutes, stirring constantly, until the mixture thickens. In a large bowl, combine the thickened cream with the fruit, pecans, orange peel, cinnamon, and cloves. Cover the filling and refrigerate until cold.

Prepare the dough: In a large bowl, combine the flour, butter, sugar, and salt. Using a pastry cutter or 2 knives, cut in the butter until the pieces are pea-sized. Add the water and mix only until the dough forms a ball. Divide the dough in half, wrap the halves tightly in plastic wrap, and flatten them slightly. Chill the dough for about 1 hour.

Preheat the oven to 375°F. On a lightly floured board, roll the dough out to a thickness of 1/8 inch. Cut the dough into rounds 4 inches in diameter. Place a level tablespoon of fruit filling slightly off-center on each pastry circle. Brush the edges of each circle with the beaten egg. Fold each pastry in half, completely enclosing the filling. Press the edges together and crimp them with the tines of a fork to seal. Lightly brush the top of each pastry turnover with beaten egg. Line 2 or 3 baking sheets with parchment paper. Place the turnovers about 1/2 inch apart on the sheets and bake them for 18 to 20 minutes, until golden.

Variation Sour Cherry Turnovers: Simmer 1 cup heavy cream with $1/4$ cup granulated sugar until slightly thickened, about 6 minutes. Stir in 1 cup dried cherries (softened in water, if needed), $1^1/2$ cups toasted chopped pecans or almonds, 1 teaspoon ground cinnamon, and $1/4$ teaspoon ground cloves. Use as the filling in the above recipe.

Triple-Chocolate Pasticiotti with Hazelnut Crust

Makes 20 pasticiotti

Traditionally, these double-crusted Italian pastries are made with a plain crust filled with ricotta, vanilla, or chocolate custard. Chef Linda Carucci's rich adaptation of her family's recipe includes semisweet chocolate, cocoa powder, and crème de cacao. Incidentally, the correct pronunciation for these triple-chocolate treats is pahs-tih-CHOH-tee.

The secret to preparing the crust is keeping the dough well chilled. You can substitute butter for the shortening if you wish. Although the texture won't be as crisp, the flavor will be richer.

CHOCOLATE HAZELNUT CRUST

4 ounces shelled hazelnuts (about 3/4 cup)

1/3 cup plus 1 tablespoon cocoa powder (preferably Dutch process)

1 1/2 cups shortening

2 cups sugar

3 eggs

2 teaspoons honey

3 cups all-purpose flour

2 teaspoons baking powder

1/4 cup confectioners' sugar

CHOCOLATE FILLING

1 3/4 cups milk

4 1/2 ounces semisweet chocolate, roughly chopped

5 egg yolks

1/4 cup sugar

1/4 cup all-purpose flour

1 tablespoon plus 2 teaspoons crème de cacao

1/2 teaspoon vanilla extract

Prepare the crust: Preheat the oven to 350°F. Toast the nuts on a baking sheet for 10 to 12 minutes. To remove the skins, place a small handful of nuts at a time in a clean kitchen towel. Fold the towel over the warm nuts and rub vigorously to loosen the skins. Let the nuts cool to room temperature before proceeding with the recipe.

Place the nuts and cocoa powder in a food processor and process until the mixture resembles ground coffee.

With an electric mixer, cream together the shortening and sugar until the mixture is light and fluffy. On low speed, add the eggs, one at a time, mixing well. Then add the honey, followed by the cocoa-hazelnut mixture. Mix on low speed just until all the ingredients are combined. Sift the flour and baking powder together directly onto the other ingredients. On low speed, mix just until the dough is smooth. Turn the dough out onto a smooth, clean work surface lightly dusted with flour and shape it into a disk. Wrap the disk with plastic wrap and refrigerate it for at least 3 hours or overnight.

Prepare the chocolate filling: In a large, heavy saucepan, heat the milk and chocolate over medium heat until the chocolate begins to melt. Remove the pan from the heat and stir the mixture until the chocolate is completely incorporated into the milk. In a large mixing bowl, whisk together the egg yolks and sugar. Add the flour, whisking until smooth. Stir in about 1 cup of the chocolate-milk mixture, blending well.

Place the saucepan with the remaining chocolate milk over medium heat and bring the milk to a boil. Remove the pan from the heat. Very slowly, pour all of the boiling chocolate milk into the egg yolk mixture, whisking constantly. Slowly pour the mixture back into the saucepan and whisk constantly over high heat just until it boils, about 1 minute. Reduce the heat to medium-low and, stirring constantly, boil gently for 2 minutes. The mixture should become shiny and have the consistency of mayonnaise.

Immediately pour the chocolate filling into a clean, shallow mixing bowl. Whisk in the crème de cacao and vanilla extract. If you are not using the filling right away, place parchment paper or plastic wrap directly on the surface of the filling and refrigerate for up to 3 days.

Assemble the pasticiotti: Lightly spray the inside of 20 fluted round metal tartlet pans (measuring about 3 inches in diameter and about $1/2$ inch deep) with nonstick pan spray. Arrange the molds on a baking sheet.

Divide the dough in half. Tightly wrap and refrigerate one half to use later for the top crusts. Divide the other half into 20 pieces and roll each into a ball about $1^1/2$ inches in diameter.

Using your thumbs and fingers, press a ball of the dough into the bottom and up the sides of each of the molds so that the dough extends about $1/8$ inch above the top edge of the mold.

When all bottom crusts are shaped, spoon 2 tablespoons of filling into each mold.

Preheat the oven to 350°F. Remove the remaining dough from the refrigerator, divide it into 20 pieces and shape each piece into a ball about $1^1/2$ inches in diameter. Roll out each ball between 2 pieces of plastic wrap into a circular shape about $1/4$ inch wider than a tart mold. Carefully peel off the top sheet of plastic wrap. Pick up the bottom sheet of plastic wrap and carefully invert and center the dough over the filled tart molds, completely covering the filling.

Using both index fingers, simultaneously press the 2 crusts together, completely sealing them. If you like, trim off any excess dough. (The dough can be combined, flattened, and baked into cookies.)

Bake for 15 to 18 minutes, until the centers of the pasticiotti are firm to the touch. Let cool for 10 minutes. Carefully invert and pry the pasticiotti from the molds, letting them cool completely on racks. Serve them bottom crust up, dusted with confectioners' sugar. Refrigerate the remaining pasticiotti for up to 2 days. Serve chilled or allow to come to room temperature.

These pastries are best baked in individual small metal tartlet shells or brioche molds. You could also bake them in mini-muffin tins.

Egg Pasta

Duck Tortellini in Brodo

Il Brodo Misto (Meat and Chicken Broth)

*Lamb Ravioli in Black Pepper Pasta
with Mushroom Tomato Sauce*

Mushroom Tomato Sauce

Seafood Ravioli with Saffron Tomato Broth

Saffron Tomato Broth

Spinach Ricotta Ravioli with Sage Butter

Fresh Pasta

Creating mouthwatering fresh pasta is child's play. All you need is a few eggs, some flour, a pinch or two of salt, and about half an hour. The one thing you don't need is a fancy mixing machine. It's best to knead pasta by hand, according to pasta expert Chef Loretta Rampone.

It's also not essential to have a pasta machine to roll out and cut the dough, although an inexpensive hand-crank model saves a lot of elbow grease. However, a lightly floured rolling pin works. So does an empty wine bottle.

Rampone uses the following rule of thumb to figure out how much pasta to make: In general, a recipe based on 4 cups of flour makes enough pasta for the following number of first-course portions:

Small filled pasta in soup for 8 people

Noodles with sauce for 4 people

Ravioli or small filled pasta with sauce for 4 people

Tortelloni, cannelloni, or lasagne noodles for 6 people

Here are some of the chef's pasta-making tips:

- *A rigid dough scraper with a handle makes it easy to scrape the table clean.*
- *Kneading the dough by hand produces the highest-quality pasta. You'll know when the dough has been kneaded enough because it will be completely smooth and elastic and won't tear if you pull it.*
- *If the dough begins to get warm before it becomes smooth, wrap it tightly in plastic and refrigerate it before continuing to knead.*
- *Never let the dough sit uncovered long enough to form a crust. Any hard pieces of dough will cause tears as you roll it out.*
- *After you've finished kneading, wrap the pasta tightly in plastic and allow it to rest about half an hour before rolling it out. Resting will relax the gluten.*
- *Avoid pulling on the pasta as you roll it out to prevent tears and crinkling during cooking. When working with the pasta sheets, it's best to lift them on the back of your hand to avoid stretching the dough and causing variations in thickness. One check for proper thinness is to hold the pasta sheet up and see if you can see light through it. Another test is to cook a piece before rolling out the rest.*
- *It's best to avoid air bubbles when making filled pastas. But if you do get one, merely poke a tiny hole near the bubble and press the air out.*

To refrigerate stuffed pasta, arrange the pasta in layers in a plastic container lined with wax paper. Sprinkle semolina or fine cornmeal flour between the layers to prevent the pasta from sticking together. Tortellini, agnolotti, cappelletti, and other stuffed pastas also freeze especially well. Simply arrange the small filled pasta on a baking sheet sprinkled with semolina flour or fine cornmeal to prevent sticking. When the pasta is frozen, place it in resealable plastic freezer bags and freeze.

To cook refrigerated pasta, drop the pasta into boiling salted water, let the water return to a boil, and cook until the pasta is just tender, about 5 minutes. To cook frozen stuffed pasta, drop the pasta directly from the freezer into boiling salted water, let the water return to a boil, and cook until the pasta floats to the surface, the dough is just tender, and the filling is hot, about 7 minutes.

Flavor egg pasta by adding one or more of the following to a recipe based on 4 cups of flour:

2 teaspoons or more finely ground black pepper, depending on how spicy you like it

1 1/2 teaspoons grated lemon zest

2 teaspoons finely chopped fresh dill

1 1/2 teaspoons finely chopped fresh sage

Egg Pasta

4 to 5 cups unbleached all-purpose flour
1/2 teaspoon salt

*4 jumbo eggs or 5 large eggs,
lightly beaten*

4 first-course servings

Measure the flour and salt directly onto a large pastry board or clean kitchen counter. With the back of a spoon, make a well in the middle of the flour. Pour the eggs into the well. Using a fork, begin beating the eggs in a clockwise motion, gradually incorporating flour from the inside of the well and taking care that the egg doesn't spill out.

When the dough is too stiff to use the fork, pull the fork out and scrape off any bits of dough, kneading them into the middle of the dough. Use a pastry or dough scraper to sweep up the flour left on the board and sift. Begin kneading the dough by hand, adding flour as necessary to form a firm but pliable dough. Continue kneading until the dough loses its craggy appearance and becomes smooth and elastic, about 10 minutes. When finished, you'll be able to stretch the dough without tearing it, and it will spring back when poked.

Form the dough into a ball, cover it tightly with plastic wrap, and let it rest for 30 minutes to relax the gluten.

Set up the pasta machine if you are using one. Divide the dough into 4 pieces. Work with one piece of dough at a time, keeping the rest covered. If the dough seems sticky, dust lightly with flour. Then feed it through the pasta machine on the widest setting, being careful not to pull or stretch the dough.

To maintain a uniform rectangular shape, fold the dough in thirds, as you would fold a letter, and press it flat to squeeze out any air bubbles. Gradually reduce the settings to create the desired thickness. The second-thinnest setting is recommended for stuffed pastas such as ravioli. As each sheet passes through the rollers for the final time, carefully lay it flat on the counter and cover it with plastic wrap. Repeat with the remaining dough.

If you use a rolling pin, divide the dough into 4 pieces and roll each piece into a ball. Cover all but 1 ball of dough with plastic wrap. Begin rolling the ball of dough from the center out, rotating the dough a quarter turn after each roll to keep it a uniform round shape. Try to roll the dough out and away from you until it is about 1/16 inch thick. Lightly dust with flour as you work, if necessary. It's important to roll the dough out quickly so it doesn't become dry and lose its elasticity.

It's difficult to specify the exact amount of flour since this will vary with the amount of moisture in the flour and the humidity in the room.

Chef's tip It's best to incorporate the flour slowly. You can always add more flour, but it's difficult, if not impossible, to save a dough that's too dry.

Use the dough immediately for stuffed pastas or wrap tightly in plastic wrap and refrigerate to stuff later.

To make ravioli: Place a 12- to 18-inch length of pasta dough on a lightly floured surface and gently fold in half lengthwise. Then unfold. Using the center crease as a guide, place about 1 to 2 teaspoons of filling just below the crease about every $2^1/2$ inches.

Either brush the dough around the filling with water or lightly spray the sheet of pasta with a fine mist of water. Fold the top half of the dough over the bottom half and press, first gently on top of the dough covering the mounds of filling, then firmly between the mounds of filling. If there are any air bubbles, use a toothpick to poke a tiny hole in the bubble and press the air out. Use a pastry wheel, sharp knife, cutter-crimper, or biscuit cutter to cut the dough into $2^1/2$-inch squares.

Alternatively, you can use a ravioli tray, which is a flat metal form with indentations for the filling and ridges that mark the ravioli edges.

To cook ravioli: Bring a pot of salted water to a boil. Add the ravioli and stir gently. After the water returns to a boil, start timing the pasta. Ravioli will take 3 to 5 minutes to cook. The best way to test for doneness is to taste one. When done, the filling will be hot and cooked through and the pasta will be tender but still firm to the bite. As soon as the ravioli are done, remove them from the water with a slotted spoon and serve them according to the recipe.

To make agnolotti: Cut the dough into 2-inch circles. Place about $1/2$ teaspoon of filling in the center of each circle. Moisten the edges and fold the dough over, forming a half-moon. Press the edges to seal.

To make tortellini: Form agnolotti, then wrap the half-moon around your finger and firmly press the points where the ends meet together.

To make cappelletti: Follow the instructions for tortellini, using 2-inch squares of dough rather than circles.

Depending on the thickness of the pasta, agnolotti, tortellini, and cappelletti will cook in about 3 minutes.

Duck Tortellini in Brodo

2 duck legs and thighs (about 2 pounds)

Salt to taste

Freshly ground black pepper to taste

1 small onion, chopped

1/2 small carrot, chopped

1/2 small stalk celery, chopped

1/2 cup unsalted or low-sodium beef,
  chicken, or duck stock

1 cup port

1 tablespoon fresh thyme leaves

1 small bay leaf

1/2 cup whole-milk ricotta

1 recipe Egg Pasta (page 123)

1 recipe Il Brodo Misto (recipe follows)

1/2 cup freshly grated Parmesan cheese

2 tablespoons minced fresh parsley
  (optional)

**About 100 tortellini,
6 to 8 first-course servings**

This recipe isn't quick, but it's absolutely delicious and worth all the effort. One time-saving tip is to use a Chinese roast duck instead of roasting your own. If you do, just cook the vegetables in a small amount of stock and port until soft. Then puree them with the duck before adding the ricotta.

Season the duck with salt and pepper. Heat a large frying pan or saucepan over medium-high heat. Cut off a small piece of duck fat and add it to the pan. Cook, stirring, until enough fat has been rendered to lightly coat the bottom of the pan. Place the duck in the pan and sear it until the skin turns golden brown, about 10 minutes. Remove the duck and discard all but 1 tablespoon of fat. Add the onion, carrot, and celery. Cook the vegetables over medium-high heat, stirring frequently, until they are tender and lightly browned, about 5 minutes.

Add the stock, port, thyme, and bay leaf. Bring the mixture to a boil. Return the duck to the pan. Cover the pan, reduce the heat to low, and cook for 30 minutes. Uncover the pan and cook about 15 minutes longer, until the meat is tender. Transfer the duck legs to a plate and set them aside until the meat is cool enough to handle. If liquid remains in the pan, increase the heat and continue cooking, stirring occasionally, until the vegetables are nearly dry. Let the vegetables cool.

Remove the duck meat from the bones. Discard the skin and save the bones for stock, if desired. Place the duck, vegetables, and ricotta in a food processor and pulse until smooth. If the filling seems too moist, add a tablespoon or two of bread crumbs made from day-old French or Italian bread. Adjust the seasoning, adding more salt or pepper, if desired.

Follow the directions on page 124 for making the tortellini.

Bring the broth to a boil. Add the tortellini and cook until they float to the surface and are tender, about 3 minutes.

Divide the tortellini and hot broth among 6 to 8 soup plates. Serve immediately, garnished with the Parmesan and parsley.

Il Brodo Misto
(Meat and Chicken Broth)

Cook the Duck Tortellini (page 125) in this richly

**Makes about 2 quarts,
6 to 8 first-course servings**

Cook the Duck Tortellini

(page 125) in this richly

flavored broth. Skimming off

any fat or foam as it rises to

the surface makes the broth

clear. The broth is also

delicious as the base for meat

and vegetable soups and the

braising liquid for stews.

1 1/2 pounds bone-in beef chuck, short ribs, shin, or shank, well rinsed

1 1/2 pounds chicken parts, such as backs and necks, well rinsed

3 quarts water

1 small onion, roughly chopped

1 small carrot, roughly chopped

1 small stalk celery, including leaves, roughly chopped

1 sprig thyme or 1/4 teaspoon dried thyme

1 bay leaf

1 whole clove

3 sprigs parsley

1/2 teaspoon whole black or white peppercorns

1/2 teaspoon salt, or to taste

Place the beef, chicken, and water in a large stockpot and bring to a boil. Skim off the fat and foam. Stir in the remaining ingredients. Reduce the heat to low and simmer, uncovered, for about 3 hours, until the broth is richly flavored. From time to time, skim off any foam that forms. In the sink, place a fine-mesh strainer over a large bowl. Carefully pour the broth through the strainer and discard the solids.

Return the strained broth to a clean stockpot and adjust the seasonings.

Lamb Ravioli in Black Pepper Pasta with Mushroom Tomato Sauce

1 teaspoon olive oil

1 pound boneless lean lamb, cut into 1-inch pieces

1 small onion, roughly chopped

1 small carrot, roughly chopped

1 small stalk celery, roughly chopped

1 cup dry red wine

1 cup low-sodium chicken or beef stock

2 teaspoons finely minced fresh rosemary

2 bay leaves

1/4 teaspoon salt

Freshly ground black pepper to taste

1/2 cup whole-milk ricotta cheese

2 tablespoons fresh goat cheese (optional)

1 recipe Egg Pasta (page 123) made with 1 tablespoon very finely ground black pepper stirred into the flour

1 recipe Mushroom Tomato Sauce (recipe follows)

48 ravioli, 8 first-course servings

Chef Loretta Rampone is known for combining unusual pastas with intriguing meat fillings and light but flavorful sauces. One of her favorite combinations is black pepper pasta stuffed with a lamb filling and served with a sauce chock full of juicy red tomatoes, earthy mushrooms, and bright green peas.

You won't find a better recipe for using lamb trimmings than this. Just be sure that the lamb is on the lean side, less than 30 percent fat.

Heat the oil in a large saucepan over high heat until nearly smoking. Add the lamb pieces and quickly brown them on all sides, about 5 minutes. Reduce the heat to medium. Add the onion, carrot, and celery and sauté for 10 minutes. Drain off any excess fat. Stir in the wine, stock, rosemary, bay leaves, salt, and pepper. Bring the mixture to a boil. Just after it boils, reduce the temperature to low, cover the pan, and simmer for about 1 hour, or until the lamb is tender. Transfer the lamb to a plate and allow it to cool. If there is any liquid left in the pan, continue cooking, stirring, until the vegetables are nearly dry. Allow the vegetables to cool.

Place the lamb, vegetables, ricotta, and goat cheese in a food processor and pulse until the mixture is smooth. Taste, adjusting the seasoning, if necessary. Use as filling for ravioli or other stuffed pasta.

Follow the directions on page 124 for making and cooking the ravioli.

Serve immediately with the Mushroom Tomato Sauce.

Mushroom Tomato Sauce

Try using a combination of wild and cultivated mushrooms for more exotic flavor.

The easiest way to peel tomatoes is to drop them in boiling water for about 30 seconds, then remove them and immediately plunge them into cold water. This hot-and-cold technique loosens the skins, making them practically slip off.

Makes about 1 quart, enough for 8 first-course or 4 to 6 entrée servings

1 tablespoon olive oil

1 teaspoon butter

1 1/2 pounds mushrooms (combination of shiitake, oyster, and cremini or other specialty mushrooms), sliced (about 8 cups)

2 shallots, minced

1 clove garlic, minced

3 cups low-sodium beef broth

1 cup port

1 tablespoon fresh thyme leaves

2 tablespoons cornstarch dissolved in 1/4 cup broth or port

3 large ripe tomatoes, peeled, seeded, and cut into 1/2-inch cubes (about 2 1/2 cups)

3/4 cup fresh or frozen peas

Salt to taste

Freshly ground black pepper to taste

In a large saucepan, heat the oil and butter over high heat. Add the mushrooms and sauté until they begin to brown and soften slightly, about 10 minutes. Add the shallots, reduce the heat to medium, and continue cooking. When the mushrooms are nicely browned, add the garlic and sauté for 2 minutes more, making sure the garlic doesn't brown. Add the broth, port, and thyme. Let the mixture simmer for 10 minutes, then add the dissolved cornstarch, stirring continually, until the sauce comes to a boil and begins to thicken. Stir in the tomatoes and peas and remove the pan from the heat. Add the salt and pepper.

Seafood Ravioli with Saffron Tomato Broth

2 tablespoons unsalted butter
1 small carrot, finely chopped
2 large shallots, finely chopped
1 small stalk celery, finely chopped
1/4 cup finely chopped fennel
1/2 cup dry white wine
1/2 teaspoon anise-flavored liqueur
    (Pernod, sambuca, or anisette)
12 large cooked shrimp, peeled and coarsely
    chopped, or 1 cup cooked bay shrimp

1 cup flaked cooked salmon
3/4 cup whole-milk ricotta cheese
1/2 cup fresh white bread crumbs
1 tablespoon finely chopped fresh parsley
1/2 teaspoon salt
1/4 teaspoon freshly ground white pepper
Pinch of cayenne pepper
1 1/2 recipes Egg Pasta (page 123)
1 recipe Saffron Tomato Broth
    (recipe follows)

54 ravioli, about 8 entrée servings

Melt the butter in a frying pan over medium-high heat. Add the carrot, shallots, celery, and fennel and cook, stirring occasionally, until the vegetables begin to soften, about 3 minutes. Add the wine and Pernod and continue cooking until all the liquid is absorbed, about 5 minutes. If the vegetables begin to brown, reduce the heat. Transfer the vegetables to a large bowl and let them cool completely.

Add the shrimp, salmon, ricotta cheese, bread crumbs, and parsley. Stir gently until thoroughly combined. Season to taste with salt and peppers. Use the mixture to fill ravioli, allowing about 1 tablespoon filling for each.

Follow the directions on page 124 for making and cooking the ravioli.

Serve immediately with the Saffron Tomato Broth.

Remember this recipe next time you're lucky enough to have some leftover poached or grilled seafood. It is delicious served with a rich saffron-scented tomato broth. The touch of Pernod and fennel gives the savory filling the flavors of Provence.

As with all stuffed pastas, it is important to use a generous hand when seasoning the filling so that it isn't overwhelmed by the pasta. A note on bread crumbs: The best bread crumbs are made by removing the crusts from day-old white bread and processing the bread in a food processor or blender.

Saffron Tomato Broth

This tantalizing, brilliant amber-colored broth is an elegant sauce for tender, plump Seafood Ravioli (page 129).

Makes 3 cups sauce, enough for 8 servings

$^1/4$ cup (4 tablespoons) unsalted butter
2 shallots, finely minced
$1^1/2$ cups fish stock or clam juice
1 cup dry white wine
$^1/4$ teaspoon saffron threads
Pinch of red pepper flakes

1 large tomato, peeled, seeded, and diced
1 cup fresh spinach leaves, washed, dried, and cut into thin shreds
1 tablespoon minced fresh basil
Salt to taste
Freshly ground black pepper to taste

Melt the butter in a frying pan over medium heat. Add the shallots and cook, stirring occasionally, until softened, about 3 minutes. Stir in the fish stock, wine, saffron, and red pepper flakes. Increase the heat to high and cook, stirring occasionally, until the liquid is reduced by half, about 5 minutes. Stir in the tomatoes, spinach, and basil and heat through. Add the salt and pepper.

Spinach Ricotta Ravioli
with Sage Butter

2 pounds fresh spinach, washed and
    stems removed

1 cup ricotta cheese

1 cup grated Parmesan cheese

1/2 cup fresh white bread crumbs

1/4 teaspoon ground nutmeg

Salt to taste

Freshly ground black pepper to taste

2 packages (1 pound each) wonton
    wrappers or 1 recipe Egg Pasta
    (page 123)

1/2 cup butter

1/4 cup tightly packed fresh sage leaves

1/2 cup chicken stock

1 cup fresh tomato or marinara sauce

1 tablespoon canola oil

Makes about 48 ravioli,
6 to 8 first-course servings

Neighborhood alimentari all over Tuscany sell a little bit of nearly every edible, including platters stacked with little balls of squeezed-out blanched spinach because spinach is used in so many recipes, especially pasta fillings and doughs. This recipe, an updated version of a classic dish, relies on a terrific time-saver: Chinese wonton wrappers. With this convenient ingredient, you can serve homemade ravioli in about 30 minutes.

To retain its vivid green color and fresh flavor, blanch the spinach in a large pot of boiling salted water, then shock it in salted ice water to stop the cooking. (Chef Rampone suggests dumping the spinach in a large strainer or colander and placing the strainer or colander in a basin of salted ice water to cool it quickly.) Then place about 1/4 cup or less of spinach at a time in a clean kitchen towel (not terrycloth) and wring out as much water as possible. Roughly chop the squeezed spinach.

Bring a large pot of water to a boil. Meanwhile, make the filling: In a large bowl, combine the chopped spinach, ricotta, 1/2 cup of the Parmesan, the bread crumbs, nutmeg, salt, and pepper; stir gently but thoroughly until well combined.

Make the wraps: Arrange 12 wonton wrappers on a clean surface. Lightly spray the wrappers with a fine mist of water. Place about 1 tablespoon of filling in the center of each wrapper. Place another wrapper on top of each one, arranging them so that the edges meet evenly. Then carefully press out the air around the mounds of filling, sealing the top wrapper to the bottom. Repeat with the remaining filling and wrappers.

Make the sauces: Melt the butter in a large frying pan over medium heat. Add the sage leaves and cook for about 1 minute, then whisk in the chicken stock. Keep the sauce warm. In a separate saucepan, heat the tomato sauce until it is warmed through.

When the pot of water is boiling, add the oil and generously salt. Carefully add the ravioli and cook them until they rise to the surface and are tender but still al dente, about 3 minutes. With a slotted spoon, remove the ravioli to a large bowl. Pour on the warm sage butter and toss gently until evenly coated.

Divide the ravioli among serving plates and garnish each with the tomato sauce. Pass the remaining Parmesan cheese at the table.

Homemade Corn Masa

Tortillas de Maiz
(Corn Tortillas)

Flour Tortillas

Carnitas

Carnitas Borrachas

Picadillo

Pollo Verde

Green Salsa

Salsa Roja de Jitomate
(Red Tomato Salsa)

Tacos Fritos

Fish Tacos Veracruz

Vegetarian Burritos de Bollos

Thai Chicken Burritos with
Rainbow Slaw and Jasmine Rice

Tandoori Chicken Lavash Roll-Ups

Kathe Kebab

Greek Salad in a Pita

Smoked Salmon Matzo Roll-Ups
with Horseradish Cream

Tortillas and
Other Flatbreads

Tortillas date back to the tenth century, during the Mayan era. Mayan cooks often hand-patted a soft corn mixture into flatbreads up to 3 feet in diameter and grilled them over hot flat stones. It wasn't until the Spanish conquistadors brought wheat flour to the Americas in the early 1500s that the idea for flour tortillas was born.

Tortillas have changed a lot since then. Nowadays the tortilla wrapping is often flavored. We have seen tortillas made with green spinach, red chile peppers, Roma tomatoes, nutty whole wheat, and numerous combinations of herbs and spices.

Fillings that traditionally included pork or beef with rice and beans now vary from Mediterranean roast vegetables to Thai chicken. Today the beans are still likely to be flavored black beans, as in the days of yore. The rice, however, is often an aromatic jasmine or basmati, a switch from the conventional long-grain variety. The salsa may be made with diced tropical fruits, as well as the more familiar diced fresh red tomatoes. It can even be a spicy peanut sauce, depending on the other flavors used. The point is that nearly any combination is possible, as long as the ingredients are high quality and fresh, and the flavors clear and bright.

If you've never had freshly made tortillas, you're missing a great taste treat. Homemade corn and flour tortillas are far superior to packaged tortillas, and they are easy to make, once you master the technique and get a rhythm going. You'll find recipes for them in this chapter, along with authentic fillings such as *carnitas* (slowly braised pork shoulder) and an unusual variation of carnitas made with dark beer, as well as *pollo verde* and a lightened *picadillo* featuring ground turkey instead of beef.

There are a number of other flatbreads besides tortillas that make delicious and convenient wraps. Try rolling tandoori chicken in Armenian lavash (page 153), tucking smoked salmon and all its classic accompaniments into softened matzo (page 156), or stuffing piquant Greek salad into pita rounds (page 155). The combination of fillings for flatbread wraps are limited only by your imagination.

Corn Tortillas

Flavorful corn tortillas are not the product of a marketing brainstorm at a snack company, but the result of thousands of years of farming and cooking in Mexico. Cultivated as early as 5500 BCE, the grassy ancestor of modern corn, *teosinte*, was slowly developed by 3000 BCE into Zea mays, a superior food crop with one major problem: it spoiled in storage. Culinary historians believe that experiments with powdered limestone as a preservative led to the "nixtamalization" of corn, a process that turned the hard corn kernels into a soft, nutritious hominy that's tasty and, when dried, easy to grind.

By the time the Spanish conquistadors arrived in the sixteenth century, the Aztec, Zapotec, and Mayan peoples had created recipes for dozens of different corn tortillas, which they used to wrap tidbits of food. Folded in half (whether crisp or soft) and stuffed, the corn tortilla becomes a *taco*. Rolled around shredded chicken and deep fried, a tortilla becomes a *flauta*, or "little flute." And when layered or rolled with meat and cheese and covered with a hearty red or green chile sauce, the tortilla literally becomes an *enchilada*, or something that's been "chilied."

For thousands of years, corn was ground by hand on stone slabs called *metates* or in large mortars called *molcajetes*, both usually made of rough volcanic stone. Luckily, there is an easy alternative in today's supermarkets in the form of corn masa mix, or *masa harina*. Just add water and stir. Most Mexican markets also carry "fresh" *masa* (dough), which may be plain or have lard added for rich tamale making. Some stores carry fresh masa in several textures: coarse for tamales, fine for tortillas, and an all-purpose medium grind that adds more texture to tortillas and makes smoother tamale dough.

Your first attempts at making tortillas will be awkward (but still fun and flavorful), so choosing the perfect masa isn't crucial. The first bag will go quickly as you gain expertise. Then you can try another brand, if you like.

In making corn tortillas, either by hand or with a tortilla press, practice is important. Make sure to keep the dough moist. Even when using fresh masa, keep a bowl of water on hand to add drops of water to each ball when patting or pressing it out. The dough must be moist enough to handle easily without cracking at the edges, but dry enough to cook quickly and not be sticky.

It's worth investing in a tortilla press if you plan to make tortillas regularly. Although heavy wooden presses are bulky and may be difficult to find, they make thin tortillas that cook quickly and evenly. Do not buy flimsy aluminum presses; they tend to break easily.

To use a tortilla press, place the masa ball between two 10- to 12-inch pieces of plastic, parchment, or wax paper. Freezer bags or other thick plastic works better than thin plastic wrap, which tends to bunch up and create a wrinkled surface. Freezer bags can be wiped off and reused.

Center the masa-plastic sandwich between the two plates of the press and close with a quick, firm push. Too gentle and slow a push leads to a thick, misshapen tortilla; too much pressure can break the press's arm and won't make the tortilla any thinner. You can either go ahead and cook this tortilla or continue pressing out the entire batch on individual plastic wrappers. The plastic will keep the tortillas moist until all the balls have been flattened.

The best cooking vessel for tortillas is a heavy cast-iron frying pan or grill pan, but any wide pan that heats evenly (including an electric skillet or pancake griddle) will work. Medium-high heat should be enough to toast each tortilla in less than a minute without the pan becoming unmanageably hot.

If the masa is good, if the heat is right, if the masa is pressed or patted to perfection, the tortilla will puff up like a golden balloon. If it doesn't, don't worry. It will still taste great. Stack the hot tortillas in a clean kitchen towel or tortilla basket.

Patting tortillas out by hand takes practice but is worthwhile because handmade tortillas are toasty and moist after cooking, with a nice light texture. Because the masa must be drier to flatten tortillas in a press without sticking, pressed tortillas have a slightly coarser texture. Try patting a masa ball between your palms with a light clapping motion, and it will flatten quickly. To get the tortilla round and evenly thin, rotate it as you pat with a slight flipping motion. A good way to practice is to take tortillas made in the press and try to make them even thinner before cooking.

Homemade Corn Masa

2 tablespoons powdered limestone
   or 3 tablespoons wood ashes
2 quarts water

1 pound dried corn (hominy, field,
   or flint)

**Makes about 2 pounds
fresh masa**

In a large nonreactive pot, mix the lime or ash with the water and add
the corn. Bring the mixture to a boil, reduce the heat to a simmer, and cook
until the corn is soft, about 20 minutes, occasionally skimming off any loose
skins. Cover the pot and let it stand overnight or at least 4 hours.

Drain and rinse the mixture. Using a food processor, food mill, or
grinder, grind the corn in small batches to make a coarse, medium, or fine
dough. To test for the proper grind, squeeze a small amount of the ground corn
between your thumb and forefinger; it will form a tiny corn tortilla with
smooth edges when ground properly. If it doesn't, regrind the mixture until
smooth.

Variations Besides making tortillas from blue corn to get a different
look and flavor, there are other ways to vary the masa. From Yucatan comes the
addition of 1 tablespoon of powdered annatto (*achiote*) seeds or 2 tablespoons
achiote recado paste to 1 pound of masa, which results in a peppery, saffron-
colored dough. A little coconut and cinnamon make tortillas mellow and sweet
and recall the flavors of Oaxaca. A teaspoon of wood ash will intensify the blue
of blue corn masa harina. One pureed beet can give a batch of dough a hot pink
hue and slight sweetness. Scraped vanilla beans, ground pine nuts or pumpkin
seeds, powdered cocoa, mashed black beans, and whole amaranth grain are
all authentic pre-Columbian additions, while roasted garlic, New Mexico chile
powder, ground coriander, ground cumin, and dried tomatoes are more modern
variations.

Make sure whatever addition you try is ground, chopped, or powdered
to a consistency appropriate to the desired fineness of the final tortilla, and try
to keep added moisture to a minimum. As long as the final masa texture is
workable, the flavor is ultimately up to you.

Tortillas de Maiz (Corn Tortillas)

Makes 12 tortillas

Mexican food maven Mark Berlin recommends doubling this recipe to allow for mistakes and appetites. As you get better at making tortillas, appetites seem to grow. You can use 1 pound finely ground fresh corn masa instead of adding water to the corn masa mix.

Note You can make the tortillas ahead of time. Just cool them completely, wrap in plastic, and refrigerate for up to a week. A quick toasting will make them soft and pliable again.

2 cups masa harina (corn masa mix)
1 to 1 1/4 cups lukewarm water

In a large bowl, thoroughly mix the masa harina and water with clean hands until well combined. The dough will feel moist, but not runny and have a smooth texture. Let the mixture stand, covered, for 10 to 15 minutes.

If you plan to press all the tortillas before cooking them, prepare 20 to 24 pieces of heavy plastic, parchment, or wax paper. Check the dough by forming a Ping-Pong-sized ball and pressing it into a small round. If it's too sticky, add a few tablespoons of masa harina. If the edges crack, especially while still small, add water, 1 tablespoon at a time, mixing well, until the dough is moist and pliable.

Divide the dough into 12 equal portions, shape them into balls and cover them with a damp kitchen towel or plastic wrap. Using both hands, shape each ball into a 6-inch round by patting it back and forth between your palms. Or place a ball between 2 plastic sheets, center it inside the tortilla press, close the press, and firmly push down the handle. Lift the handle and remove the tortilla. Peel away 1 layer of plastic, lay the tortilla gently across your outstretched palm, and carefully peel away the other piece of plastic.

Heat the frying pan on medium-high until it is hot enough for a water drop to sizzle and dance. Lay each tortilla in the hot pan for about 30 seconds, or until the edges dry visibly and curl up slightly. Use your fingers or a spatula to flip gently and let the second side cook for 20 to 30 seconds, or until the tortilla puffs up or is just toasted. Stack the hot tortillas in a clean kitchen towel or tortilla basket. Serve warm.

Flour Tortillas

4 cups unbleached all-purpose flour

1 teaspoon salt

2 teaspoons baking powder

^{1}/8 to ^{2}/3 cup lard or shortening

1 to 1^1/2 cups warm water

In a medium bowl, use a fork or whisk to combine the flour, salt, and baking powder. Cut the lard into the flour with a fork or pastry blender (this can also be done in a food processor with several brief pulses). Mound the flour on a clean countertop, make a well in the center of the mound, and add the water, a spoonful at a time, until a soft but not sticky dough is formed.

Knead the dough in the bowl or on a lightly floured surface just until it is smooth. Then cover it and set aside for 10 to 20 minutes. For average (6-inch) tortillas, form into 18 small balls about 1^1/2 inches in diameter. Cover until you are ready to flatten them.

Flatten the balls of dough by patting them between the palms of your hands. Then, on a lightly floured surface, roll them out into rounds about 6 inches in diameter and ^{1}/8 inch thick. Cook the tortillas immediately. If you choose to flatten them all at once before cooking, be sure to stack them between sheets of plastic.

Cook the tortillas right away, without refrigerating them. Heat a frying pan on medium-high until it is hot enough for a water drop to sizzle and dance. One at a time, lay each tortilla in the hot pan for about 30 seconds, or until it puffs or bubbles slightly. Use your fingers or a spatula to flip gently and let the second side cook for 20 to 30 seconds, or until the tortilla puffs up or is just toasted. As they finish cooking, wrap the hot tortillas in a clean kitchen towel.

Note Although some shortening is needed for flakiness, the recipe will work with as little as 2 tablespoons if you want a lower-fat tortilla.

Makes about 18 tortillas

Until the relatively recent popularity of burritos ("little donkeys"), flour tortillas were found only in the Southwest and parts of northern Mexico. Homemade flour tortillas are thicker and flakier than the ones used in burrito shops, good enough to eat plain (or buttered) and much better than store-bought tortillas for mopping up a good chile stew.

Because the dough is so pliable, flour tortillas can be rolled out to any size that will fit in your frying pan or griddle. Rolling them out is better than using a tortilla press because the gluten in the flour prevents pressing them thin enough. The cooking surface should be dry and fairly hot, but not quite as hot as for corn tortillas. A little scorching, leaving dark spots, gives flour tortillas a great toasty flavor.

Carnitas

3 pounds pork shoulder or butt, skin and bone removed
Salt to taste (1 to 3 teaspoons)

Cut the pork into 2- to 3-inch cubes. Place the pork in a large, heavy pot and toss it with the salt. Barely cover the pork with cold water and bring the water to a boil, uncovered. Occasionally skim off any foam that forms. Reduce the heat to medium and simmer, uncovered, without stirring, until most of the water has evaporated and the pork fat begins to render out, 1 1/2 to 2 hours.

When the pork begins to brown, reduce the heat to low. Continue to cook, stirring occasionally, for 45 minutes to 1 hour, until the meat is well browned, crispy, and beginning to shred. Use the carnitas immediately or allow to cool, then cover and refrigerate for up to 3 days.

Carnitas Borrachas

3 pounds pork shoulder or butt, skin and
  bone removed

Salt to taste (1 to 3 teaspoons)

12 ounces dark beer, preferably Mexican

2 to 4 tablespoons New Mexico or
  California chile powder

**Makes enough for 6 entrées,
or 12 to 16 appetizer portions**

Chef Mark Berlin discovered

this sensational recipe at a

taco stand in Puerto Vallarta.

Cut the pork into 2- to 3-inch cubes. Place the pork in a large, heavy pot and toss it with the salt and beer. Barely cover the pork with cold water and bring the water to a boil. Occasionally skim off any foam that forms. Reduce the heat to medium and simmer, uncovered, without stirring, until most of the water has evaporated and the pork fat begins to render out, about 2 hours.

When the pork begins to brown, reduce the heat to low and stir in the chile powder. Cook, stirring occasionally, for 45 minutes to 1 hour, until the meat is well browned, crispy, and beginning to shred. Use immediately or allow to cool, then cover and refrigerate for up to 3 days.

Picadillo

This sweet, spiced meat preparation is found in all Spanish-influenced cuisines. In Argentina, hard-cooked eggs are often added after the spicy beef mixture has cooled. In Spain, pork is the meat of choice, and vinegar and tomatoes are often added as seasonings. Picadillo is a perfect filling for tortillas and empanadas.

1 cup currants or raisins

1 cup dry sherry or marsala, or 1 cup apple juice mixed with 2 teaspoons sherry or cider vinegar

1 tablespoon olive oil or pan spray (optional)

1 large onion, minced

2 pounds lean ground turkey, chicken, pork, beef, or a combination

2 to 4 garlic cloves, minced

1 teaspoon ground cinnamon

1 teaspoon ground cumin

1 teaspoon freshly ground black pepper

1/2 teaspoon ground cloves

1/2 cup pitted green olives, sliced

Salt to taste (amount will depend on saltiness of olives)

In a small saucepan, bring the currants and sherry to a boil. Remove the pan from the heat and set it aside.

In a large frying pan, heat the oil over medium-high heat. Add the onion and sauté for 5 minutes or until it is translucent. Add the meat and cook, stirring to break it up, until lightly browned. Add the garlic and sauté 1 minute longer.

Stir in the cinnamon, cumin, pepper, cloves, olives, salt, and sherry-soaked currants. Simmer the mixture over medium heat until the liquid has thickened slightly, about 10 minutes.

Use the picadillo immediately as a filling for tacos or burritos or cover and refrigerate for up to 3 days.

Pollo Verde

1 whole fryer chicken (about 3 1/2 pounds),
  rinsed

4 onions, unpeeled

2 heads of garlic

2 carrots, coarsely chopped

2 stalks celery, coarsely chopped

1 tablespoon whole coriander seeds

1 tablespoon black peppercorns

2 tablespoons olive oil

1 tablespoon ground cumin

1 teaspoon ground coriander

1 pound tomatillos, husked, rinsed, and
  quartered (about 4 cups)

1 1/2 pounds green chiles, roasted, peeled,
  seeded, and chopped

Salt to taste

**Makes enough for 6 entrées
or 12 to 16 appetizer portions**

For this recipe, try
Anaheim, New Mexico,
poblano, or any other large
pepper (including bell), or
any combination of chiles.

To roast chiles or tomatoes,
use long tongs to turn them
over an open flame (burner,
broiler, or grill) until the skins
have completely blistered.
Or cut them in half lengthwise, place on lightly greased
baking sheets, and roast in a
500°F oven or under an
electric broiler. Place charred
peppers in a paper bag until
cool enough to handle. Then
remove the skins, seeds, and
stems using a sharp paring
knife. A small bowl of water
can be helpful for rinsing
blackened skins off your
fingers. If working with really
hot chiles, you may want to
wear gloves.

Place the chicken in a large nonreactive pot, add just enough water to cover it, and bring the water to a boil. Skim off any foam or fat that appears on the surface and reduce the heat to a simmer.

Rinse the onions, then cut 1/2 inch off each end. Cut the onions in half lengthwise and peel them. Add these trimmings to the pot. Coarsely chop the peeled onions and set them aside.

Remove and set aside 6 to 9 large cloves from the garlic heads. Coarsely chop the rest of the garlic and add to the pot along with the carrots, celery, coriander seeds, and peppercorns. Simmer the mixture, uncovered, until the chicken is fully cooked (when a leg joint easily comes apart), 40 to 45 minutes.

Use tongs to remove the chicken to a large plate or bowl and let it cool. Remove and discard the skin and pull the chicken apart to speed cool-ing. Remove the meat from bones and pull it apart into bite-size pieces; set aside. Return the bones to the pot and continue simmering the stock for about 1 hour. Remove the stock from the heat and strain it, discarding the bones and vegetables; let the stock cool. Peel and chop the reserved garlic cloves.

In a 3-quart saucepan, heat the oil over high heat. Add the chopped onions and sauté for 5 minutes, or until they are translucent. Stir in the cumin, ground coriander, and garlic and reduce the heat to medium-high. Stir in the tomatillos and sauté for 2 minutes. Stir in the chiles, chicken, and salt and add enough stock to cover. Reduce the heat to a simmer and cook, uncovered, until almost dry, 20 to 30 minutes, stirring occasionally. Refrigerate the remaining stock for up to 5 days or freeze it for up to 3 months and use as a base for enchilada sauce, soup, or other recipes.

Green Salsa

Makes about 3 cups

Here's proof that salsa doesn't have to be spicy to be good. Tomatillos, which look like small green tomatoes covered with a tight-fitting papery husk, add hints of lemon and apple flavors to this quick salsa.

6 tomatillos, husked, washed, and quartered

3 poblano chiles, 5 Anaheim chiles, or 2 bell peppers (about ¹/2 pound), cored and seeded

1 bunch scallions, trimmed and coarsely chopped

1 cup coarsely chopped fresh cilantro

Juice and grated zest of 2 limes

2 to 4 tablespoons olive oil

Salt to taste

1 clove garlic, coarsely chopped (optional)

Place all the ingredients in a food processor or blender. Process until they are well blended. Use the salsa immediately to garnish tacos, burritos, or tamales or refrigerate it for up to 3 days.

Salsa Roja de Jitomate
(Red Tomato Salsa)

2 to 6 serrano or jalapeño chiles, roasted,
   peeled, and diced

3 cloves garlic, chopped

2 to 4 tablespoons olive, peanut,
   or safflower oil

Salt to taste

1 1/2 pounds tomatoes, roasted, peeled,
   and diced

Makes about 3 cups

Use a food processor, blender, or molcajete to coarsely grind the chiles and garlic with the oil and salt. Then add the tomatoes and process just enough to combine the ingredients but not enough to create a puree. Transfer the mixture to a nonreactive saucepan bring it to a boil. Cook for 1 to 5 minutes, depending on how watery the tomatoes are, until the mixture reaches the consistency of a sauce but has not thickened. Remove the sauce from the heat and let it cool. Serve at room temperature with tacos, tamales, or burritos. Store in the refrigerator for up to 3 days.

When the Aztecs went to market, they could choose from tomatoes in dozens of colors, shapes, and flavors. They often turned tomatoes into sauces by grinding them in a molcajete. Within just a few years of conquering Mexico, the Spanish introduced a tomato sauce much like this one to the cooks of Naples and changed the course of culinary history.

Tacos

A taco is nothing more than a tortilla wrapped around a filling. Tacos can be fried, baked, or simply made by toasting a tortilla over a flame or in a hot frying pan and filling it with leftovers and salsa.

One easy way to make enough tacos for a large crowd is to place tortillas flat on baking sheets, smear each with some refried beans, add a spoonful of grilled meat or sautéed vegetables, and sprinkle with cheese. Just 5 minutes in a hot oven and a dozen tacos can be ready to top with shredded cabbage and cilantro and served. Children love plain quesadillas (cheese tacos) made this way.

Cheese isn't essential to a taco. When it is used, it's in moderation. Queso Chihuahua, which is similar to a full-flavored Monterey Jack, is sometimes used because it melts easily. Cotija, which is salty like feta, is sometimes crumbled on top.

Street vendors in Mexico make tacos of all types—roast pork, pollo verde, tongue, prawns, and grilled beef—using either a grill, a fryer, or a *comal* or a combination of these.

Tacos Fritos

4 corn tortillas

4 ounces cheese (such as cheddar, Monterey
    Jack, queso fresco, or mozzarella), sliced
    or shredded

3/4 cup refried or mashed black or pinto
    beans

1/2 pound cooked meat (pollo verde,
    picadillo, carnitas, or grilled chicken
    or fish), sliced or shredded

1/2 cup chopped red onion

Salsa, shredded cabbage or lettuce, and
    cilantro, for garnish

Makes 4 tacos, 2 servings

Try different combinations of fillings following the basic steps of this recipe. Use 2 pans or a large griddle to cook for a crowd.

Lightly spray a large frying pan with nonstick pan spray or grease with oil or shortening. Heat on high until very hot. Lay the tortillas in the pan so that they curve up the sides of the pan and meet in the center without much overlap.

Lay equal amounts of cheese, beans, meat, and onion in the center of each tortilla and fold the outside edge to the center. Use a fork to move all the tacos to the hottest area of the pan, and let them cook until the cheese begins to melt and the tortilla is crisp. Flip each tortilla with a fork and cook it until the second side is crisp. Serve hot, garnished with salsa, cabbage, and cilantro.

Fish Tacos Veracruz

Makes 12 tacos

This is a fast, easy, and
delicious recipe.

2 pounds red snapper fillets

2 tablespoons olive oil

4 cloves garlic, finely minced

1 zucchini, cut in half lengthwise and sliced
    1/4 inch thick (about 1 1/2 cups)

2 tomatoes, cut into 1/2-inch chunks
    (about 2 cups)

1 bunch scallions, including green tops,
    sliced 1/4 inch thick (about 1 1/2 cups)

6 serrano chiles, seeded and chopped,
    or to taste

Juice of 1 lime

1 tablespoon ground coriander

1 tablespoon chopped fresh marjoram

1 tablespoon chopped fresh thyme

1 teaspoon salt

1 teaspoon freshly ground black pepper

1/2 teaspoon ground allspice

12 corn tortillas

2 cups grated manchego or extra-sharp
    cheddar cheese

Cilantro sprigs and salsa, for garnish

In a bowl, toss the fish fillets with the oil and garlic. Let stand for 10 minutes or refrigerate for up to 3 hours.

In a separate, nonreactive bowl, toss the zucchini, tomatoes, scallions, chiles, lime juice, coriander, marjoram, thyme, salt, pepper, and allspice. Let stand for 10 minutes or refrigerate for up to 3 hours.

Preheat the oven to 500°F. Place the fish and vegetable mixtures in a single layer in a large nonreactive baking pan and bake for 8 minutes, uncovered, until the fish flakes easily. Cover to keep warm.

Spread the tortillas on baking sheets so that they barely overlap. Sprinkle about 2 tablespoons of cheese on each and toast them in the hot oven for 2 minutes, until the cheese melts. (This may be done in several batches.)

Spoon about 1/3 cup of the warm fish mixture onto the center of each tortilla. Garnish with cilantro. Fold while the tortilla is still warm and serve with salsa.

Vegetarian Burritos de Bollos

2 cups shredded winter squash (such as
    butternut or Hubbard) or garnet yams

2 cups cooked jasmine or other
    long-grain rice

1 bunch scallions, including tops, thinly
    sliced (about 1 1/2 cups)

6 cloves garlic, minced

1 poblano or 2 Anaheim chiles, seeded and
    finely chopped

1/2 cup crumbled cotija or grated Romano
    cheese

1 tablespoon ground cumin

3 eggs

3 teaspoons salt

Oil for frying or nonstick pan spray

2 medium tomatoes, chopped

1 large red onion, chopped

1/2 cup chopped fresh cilantro

Juice of 1 lime

2 to 6 chopped jalapeño chiles
    (seeded or not, depending on
    desired spiciness)

12 (10- to 12-inch) flour tortillas

1 can (16 ounces) refried beans

2 cups shredded Monterey Jack cheese

Makes 12 burritos

These crisp vegetable patties are delicious served alone with salsa or in corn tortillas for tacos or rolled in flour tortillas for burritos.

Chef's note After peeling the hard squash or yam, shred by hand using a mandoline or the coarse shredding blade of a four-sided grater. Or shred in the food processor.

Chile peppers vary greatly in heat. To check, cut the stem end off and touch it to your tongue. You'll know right away how hot the pepper will be. To tame the heat, remove the seeds and inner white membranes. And if you like the flavor and crunch of chile peppers but don't want the heat, substitute Anaheim or bell peppers.

Preheat the oven to 450°F. In a bowl, thoroughly combine the squash, rice, scallions, garlic, poblanos, cotija cheese, cumin, eggs, and 2 teaspoons of the salt. With your hands, form the mixture into twenty-four 2-inch patties.

Heat a small amount of oil in a large frying pan over medium-high heat or spray the pan with nonstick pan spray. Fry the patties for about 3 minutes on each side, until they are crisp and brown. Add more oil to the pan, if necessary. Drain the cooked patties on paper towels.

In a bowl, combine the tomatoes, onion, cilantro, lime juice, remaining 1 teaspoon salt, and jalapeños. Spread the tortillas on several baking sheets, trying not to overlap them too much. Top each tortilla with about 2 tablespoons of the refried beans and 2 tablespoons of the Jack cheese. Toast the tortillas in the oven for about 2 minutes, until the cheese melts. (This may be done in several batches.) Place 2 vegetable patties and 2 tablespoons of the tomato mixture on each tortilla while it is still warm. Fold the two opposite sides over the filling so that they overlap about 1 inch, then roll up like a jelly roll.

Thai Chicken Burritos with Rainbow Slaw and Jasmine Rice

Makes 6 servings

We've sampled East-West, Tex-Mex, Cal-Ital fusion dishes. It was only a matter of time before innovative chefs merged two of today's most popular cuisines: Thai and Mexican.

To toast sesame or other seeds, place them in a dry frying pan and cook over low heat, stirring or shaking the pan occasionally, until the seeds become fragrant and turn light brown.

PEANUT SAUCE
15 sprigs cilantro

4 cloves garlic

1 tablespoon minced fresh ginger

$2/3$ cup crunchy peanut butter, preferably natural

$1/4$ cup soy sauce

$1/4$ cup unseasoned rice vinegar

$1/4$ cup plus 2 tablespoons unsweetened coconut milk

2 tablespoons brown sugar

1 tablespoon peanut, canola, or safflower oil

1 teaspoon chile oil

RAINBOW SLAW
$1/4$ head of red cabbage, thinly sliced

1 teaspoon kosher salt

$1/4$ head of Napa cabbage, thinly sliced

2 carrots, shredded

1 red bell pepper, seeded and diced

2 tablespoons finely chopped fresh cilantro (about 10 sprigs)

1 scallion, trimmed and finely chopped

$1/4$ cup unseasoned rice vinegar

2 tablespoons sugar

1 tablespoon canola oil

$1/2$ teaspoon sesame oil, preferably Asian

$1/4$ teaspoon chile oil

Salt to taste

Freshly ground black pepper to taste

1 tablespoon toasted sesame seeds

JASMINE RICE
$1^1/4$ cups chicken stock

$3/4$ cup unsweetened coconut milk

3 cloves garlic, minced

1 cup Jasmine rice, rinsed, or long-grain rice

Pinch of salt

THAI CHICKEN
1 pound boneless, skinless chicken thighs, cut into $3/4$-inch pieces

6 (10- to 12-inch) flour tortillas

$1^1/2$ teaspoons sesame seeds, toasted (optional)

Prepare the peanut sauce: Place the cilantro, garlic, and ginger in a food processor and process until the ingredients are minced fine. Add the peanut butter, soy sauce, vinegar, coconut milk, brown sugar, peanut oil, and chile oil. Continue processing until the mixture is smooth. Refrigerate the sauce for up to 3 days.

Prepare the slaw: In a colander, toss together the red cabbage and kosher salt. Set aside for 15 minutes, until the cabbage is softened; squeeze out any liquid. In a large bowl, combine the red cabbage with the Napa cabbage, carrots, bell pepper, cilantro, and scallion.

In another bowl, combine the vinegar, sugar, canola oil, sesame oil, and chile oil. Pour the dressing over the cabbage mixture and season with salt and pepper. Set the slaw aside in the refrigerator and toss occasionally to blend the flavors. Toss in the sesame seeds just before serving. The slaw can be refrigerated for up to 3 days.

Prepare the jasmine rice: In a medium saucepan, combine the chicken stock, coconut milk, and garlic. Bring the liquid to a boil. Stir in the rice and salt. Cover, reduce the heat to a simmer, and cook for 20 minutes. Remove the pan from the heat and let it stand for 10 minutes. Fluff the rice with a fork before serving.

Prepare the Thai chicken: In a nonreactive bowl, combine the chicken and $1/2$ cup of the peanut sauce. Cover the bowl and let the chicken marinate in the refrigerator for at least 30 minutes or up to 24 hours.

When you are ready to cook the chicken, preheat the broiler. Drain the marinade from the chicken and discard it. Place the chicken pieces in a single layer on a broiler pan and broil them, turning once, until the chicken is golden brown and cooked through, about 8 minutes.

Meanwhile, lightly sprinkle a few drops of water on a tortilla. Heat a dry nonstick frying pan over high heat. Place the tortilla in the hot pan and toast it, turning it once or twice, until it is warm and pliable. Place the warm tortilla on a flat work surface.

Spread $1/2$ cup of hot cooked rice in a strip across the center of the tortilla. Top the rice with $1/3$ cup of chicken. Drizzle 1 tablespoon of the peanut sauce over the chicken and rice. Spoon $1/2$ cup of slaw on top of that.

Bring the bottom edge of the tortilla over the ingredients, enclosing them snugly. Fold in the sides and roll the tortilla to completely enclose all the ingredients. Repeat with the remaining ingredients.

Serve each burrito on a plate, drizzled with 1 tablespoon peanut sauce and sprinkled with $1/4$ teaspoon toasted sesame seeds.

Tandoori Chicken Lavash Roll-Ups

Makes 36 pieces for hors d'oeuvres or 6 sandwich servings, two 3-inch rolls per person

These make-ahead portable sandwiches utilize the soft fresh lavash bread found in Middle Eastern markets or in the deli section of large supermarkets. Lavash is available in a variety of sizes and shapes. If you deviate from the dimensions specified, just adjust the amount of ingredients accordingly.

For authentic and optimum flavor, it's best to toast and grind whole coriander and cumin seeds, although you can substitute ground spices to save time.

TANDOORI MARINADE

1 tablespoon coriander seeds or ground coriander

1 1/4 teaspoons cumin seeds or ground cumin

1 tablespoon minced fresh ginger

3 cloves garlic, minced

1 1/2 teaspoons kosher salt

1/4 teaspoon turmeric

1/4 teaspoon cayenne pepper

1/8 teaspoon ground cinnamon

Pinch of ground cloves

Pinch of ground nutmeg

3/4 cup plain yogurt

1 teaspoon fresh lemon juice

1 pound boneless, skinless chicken thighs, cut into 1-inch strips (about 7 thighs)

2 packages (3 ounces each) processed cream cheese (not "natural" cream cheese), at room temperature

1/4 cup mango chutney

2 pieces soft fresh lavash bread, each about 18×11 inches

1 cup fresh mint leaves

1 English cucumber (about 8 ounces), unpeeled, cut in half lengthwise and sliced 1/4 inch thick

6 large red radishes, finely julienned, or 1/2 cup radish sprouts

3 cups hearts of romaine lettuce, cut into fine shreds

Make the tandoori marinade: In a small frying pan, toast the coriander and cumin seeds together over medium-high heat until the seeds brown and release their fragrance, about 1 to 2 minutes. Immediately transfer the toasted seeds to a mortar or spice grinder to pulverize them. Transfer the ground seeds to a food processor. Add the ginger, 1/3 teaspoon of the garlic, 1/2 teaspoon of the salt, the turmeric, cayenne, cinnamon, ground cloves, nutmeg, and about 1/4 cup of the yogurt. Process until the mixture forms a smooth puree, scraping down the sides of the work bowl as necessary. Add the lemon juice and the remaining yogurt. Process until the ingredients are combined thoroughly. Spoon 3 tablespoons of the marinade into a small jar and refrigerate it.

Pour the remaining marinade into a bowl. Stir in the chicken strips and refrigerate the mixture for up to 24 hours, stirring occasionally. Transfer the chicken and marinade to a colander and allow the excess marinade to drain off. Discard the used marinade.

Spray a large frying pan, stovetop griddle, or grill pan with nonstick pan spray and heat the pan over medium-high heat. When the pan is hot, grill the marinated chicken strips, being careful not to crowd them, just until cooked through, about 3 minutes on each side. Set the cooked chicken aside to cool.

In a small bowl, mix together the cream cheese, chutney, remaining garlic, remaining 1 teaspoon salt, and 3 tablespoons of reserved tandoori marinade. (The cream cheese has a tendency to break down and become very runny when this spread is prepared in a food processor. It's best to blend the ingredients by hand.)

To assemble: Lay a sheet of lavash on a flat surface with one of the longer sides closest to you. Spread half of the mango chutney spread over the entire surface of the lavash except a 3/4-inch margin along the bottom edge. Lay 2 rows of mint leaves side by side across the bottom of the lavash on top of the chutney spread. Lay half of the grilled chicken strips across the lavash directly on top of the lower row of mint leaves. Next lay half of the cucumber slices side by side directly on top of the upper row of mint leaves, followed by half of the radish julienne on top of the cucumber slices and then half of the lettuce, extending the lettuce onto the spread by about 2 inches.

To roll the lavash: Using both hands, fold the bottom 3/4-inch margin up onto the chicken. Keep that fold in place and, as tightly as possible, roll the lavash away from you toward the opposite side, smoothing out the roll and tucking in any stray pieces of filling that pop out. The spread at the opposite end will keep the roll sealed. Place a sheet of plastic wrap about 8 inches longer than the lavash on a flat surface and center the rolled lavash on the wrap. Tightly roll the sandwich "cylinder" in the wrap, twist each end of the wrap, and fold the ends onto the seam side of the lavash roll to seal. Refrigerate the wrap, seam side down, for about 1 1/2 to 8 hours. Repeat with the remaining ingredients to make a second roll.

To serve as an hors d'oeuvre, remove the plastic wrap and place the rolled lavash on a cutting board. Use a serrated knife to cut 1-inch slices; to ensure "clean" slices, be sure to wipe the knife with paper towels before making each slice. Serve the pieces, filling side up, on a plate. To serve the roll-ups as sandwiches, cut each roll into six 3-inch pieces.

For an attractive presentation, arrange bite-size pieces of the roll-ups in a large basket or serving platter lined with leaves of red chard or red leaf lettuce. Garnish with black and pimiento-stuffed olives, fresh sprigs of mint or coriander, and well-drained colorful pickled vegetables.

Kathe Kebab

Makes 6 servings

This spicy filling rolled in grilled flour tortillas may remind you of an Indian version of chimichangas (fried filled flour tortillas). Top the chicken with shredded lettuce or sprigs of cilantro, if you desire, before rolling the Kathe kebab up.

1/2 cup canola oil

1 red onion, thinly sliced

1 1/2 pounds boneless, skinless chicken, cut into 1/2-inch cubes

1 1/2-inch piece of ginger, peeled and grated

4 cloves garlic, minced

1 large ripe tomato, cut into 1/2-inch cubes

1 jalapeño chile, minced

1 1/2 tablespoons ground coriander

2 teaspoons garam masala

2 teaspoons mango powder (or substitute 1 tablespoon lemon juice)

1 1/2 teaspoons ground cumin

1/4 teaspoon asafetida or heeng

1/4 teaspoon cayenne pepper, or to taste

Salt to taste

6 (10- to 12-inch) flour tortillas

1 lemon, cut into 6 wedges

In a large frying pan, heat about 1/3 cup of the oil over medium-high heat. Add 3/4 of the onion slices and cook, stirring occasionally, until they are softened and browned, about 10 minutes. Add the chicken and cook, stirring, until the chicken is no longer pink, about 5 minutes. Then stir in the ginger, garlic, tomato, and jalapeño. Reduce the heat to low and cook about 5 minutes longer.

In a separate frying pan, heat the remaining oil over medium-high heat. Add the coriander, garam masala, mango powder, cumin, asafetida, cayenne, and salt and cook, stirring, for a minute or two to bring out the flavor of the spices. Stir the seasonings into the chicken.

Preheat a stovetop griddle or large frying pan over medium-high heat. Put a small amount of oil in the pan. Add a flour tortilla and cook it for about 1 minute to toast the bottom of the tortilla, then remove it from the heat. Spoon about 1 cup of the chicken filling in the middle of the tortilla. Sprinkle with about 1/6 of the remaining onions and the juice from a lemon wedge. Use a wide spatula to roll up the tortilla. Repeat with the remaining ingredients. Serve warm.

Greek Salad in a Pita

1/2 head of romaine lettuce, cut into fine shreds (about 3 cups)

2 large ripe tomatoes, cut into thin wedges (about 2 cups)

1/2 small red onion, thinly sliced (about 1/2 cup)

1/2 English cucumber, cut lengthwise into quarters and sliced 1/2 inch thick (about 2 cups)

1 red bell pepper, seeded and julienned (about 1 1/2 cups)

4 ounces pitted Kalamata olives (1/2 cup)

8 ounces feta cheese

Freshly ground black pepper to taste

1/4 cup red wine vinegar or lemon juice

2 teaspoons chopped fresh oregano or 1 teaspoon dried

1 cup olive oil

Salt to taste

6 large or 12 snack-size pitas

Middle Eastern pocket bread is a convenient wrap for your favorite salad. We especially love it with Greek salad, a zesty and colorful mélange of crisp romaine and cucumbers with juicy red tomatoes, sweet red peppers, piquant Kalamata olives, and tangy white feta cheese. A word about feta: It's always best to ask for a taste before buying. Cured feta varies considerably in texture, flavor, and saltiness, ranging from mellow and creamy to sharp and crumbly.

Wash the lettuce, spin it dry, and set it aside. In a large bowl, combine the tomatoes, onion, cucumber, pepper, and olives. Cut half of the cheese into 1/4-inch cubes and toss into the vegetables. Season the mixture with a few turns of the peppermill or sprinkle with about 1/4 teaspoon ground pepper.

Pour the vinegar into a food processor. Crumble the remaining feta cheese into the processor and add the oregano. With the processor running, slowly drizzle in the oil to make a smooth dressing. Taste and add salt, if necessary.

Toss 1/2 cup of the dressing with the vegetables and set the vegetable mixture aside for at least 20 minutes or refrigerate it for up to 4 hours.

To assemble: In a medium bowl, lightly toss the remaining dressing with the lettuce. Heat the pita, if you like, for a few minutes in a warm oven. For large pitas, cut a slice about 1/2 inch from the top. Carefully open up the bread rounds. Spoon about 1/2 cup dressed romaine and 3/4 cup of the vegetable mixture into each pita. For smaller pitas, cut them in half and fill them with the romaine and vegetables.

Smoked Salmon Matzo Roll-Ups with Horseradish Cream

Makes 6 rolled sandwiches or 36 hors d'oeuvres

Don't overlook matzo as an interesting flatbread to wrap around any number of fillings. These portable sandwich rolls are easy to make but should be served within a few hours to prevent them from getting too soggy.

6 pieces matzo

1 package (8 ounces) cream cheese, at room temperature

2 teaspoons fresh lemon juice

1 teaspoon prepared horseradish

1 teaspoon grated lemon zest

1/2 cup mayonnaise

1 tablespoon chopped fresh dill

2 tablespoons nonpareil capers, rinsed and drained

1/4 teaspoon salt

Pinch of freshly ground black pepper

1 large ripe tomato

4 1/2 ounces smoked salmon or gravlax, thinly sliced

1/2 sweet onion, cut into 1/4-inch cubes

8 fresh chives or 6 scallion tops

Place a clean kitchen towel on a flat work surface. Cover the towel with a sheet of plastic wrap. Wet both sides of each matzo under cold running water and lay the wet matzos side by side on the plastic wrap. Cover with a sheet of plastic wrap and place a second clean kitchen towel on top. Tuck the sides of the kitchen towel under the matzos and let them stand for 45 minutes, until they are soft and pliable enough to be rolled up loosely. If necessary, sprinkle a little more water over each matzo, cover them again, and let them stand 10 minutes longer.

In a bowl, combine the cream cheese, lemon juice, horseradish, and lemon zest and beat by hand just until the cream cheese is smooth. Stir in the mayonnaise, dill, capers, salt, and pepper until the mixture is well blended.

Cut the tomato into 1/4-inch-thick slices. Then cut the slices in half.

Place a softened matzo on a piece of plastic wrap on a work surface so that the perforations run perpendicular to the edge of the counter. Spread 1/4 cup of the cream cheese mixture evenly on the matzo, being sure to cover the entire surface. Place a slice or two of the smoked salmon in a horizontal strip about 1/2 inch up from the bottom of the matzo. Place 3 half-slices of tomato on top of the salmon, alternating the half-rounds so that the tomatoes completely cover the salmon.

Place 1 tablespoon of the chopped onion in a strip alongside the salmon. Place 3 chives on top of the onion. (Or cut a scallion top lengthwise into 1/4-inch strips and place it on top of onion.)

Using the plastic wrap to help you, start rolling up the matzo, beginning with the edge closest to you. Roll as tightly as possible, tucking in any stray filling as you go. Wipe off any cream cheese mixture that may have oozed out and wrap the matzo roll tightly in plastic wrap, twisting the ends. Repeat with remaining matzos and fillings. Refrigerate the rolls, seam side down, for 1 hour before serving.

To serve as an hors d'oeuvre or snack, remove the plastic wrap. Using a serrated knife, cut each matzo roll into 6 slices. Place the slices on their cut sides on a platter and serve immediately. To serve as rolled sandwiches, untwist the plastic wrap at one end and roll it down as you eat. Always serve this dish well chilled.

Basic Tamale Masa from Masa Harina

Classic Pork Tamales

Yucatan Chicken Bundles

Steamed Fish with Coconut

Coco-Cocoa Tamales

Banana Leaves Stuffed with Fruited Rice

Corned Beef and Cabbage Rolls

Garlic Chicken Cabbage Rolls

Smoked Salmon with Cabbage Leaves

Eggplant, Roasted Red Pepper,
and Goat Cheese Roulade

Red Pepper Vinaigrette

Dolmas Stuffed with Bulgar
and Roasted Garlic

Herb-Stuffed Turkey Dolmas

Mustard Greens Filled with Jambalaya

Niçoise Salad in Butter
Lettuce Wrappers

Pick-Up Caesar Salads

Lamb Dolmas Agrodolce

Romaine Leaves Stuffed with Cobb Salad

Cobb Salad Dressing

Potato Chip Cones

Russet Potato Pancakes Stuffed
with Cheddar Cheese and Scallions

Vegetable Wraps

Throughout the Mediterranean, leaves and other vegetables are favorite "wrappers" because they provide moisture, delicate flavor, and are easy to form into neat packages. The Turkish word for "stuffed" is *dolmas*. Palace food during the Ottoman Empire, dolmas or stuffed grape leaves are commonplace today. But they don't have to taste ordinary. Try stuffing them with bulgur and roasted garlic or with ground lamb and the sweet and sour flavors of North Africa.

In addition to grape leaves, you can stuff savory fillings into lettuce, cabbage, spinach, chard, or mustard greens. For example, jambalaya, a signature Creole dish of seasoned rice cooked with chicken, ham, and smoked pork, is a perfect match for spicy mustard greens. Our variation of corned beef and cabbage features crispy corned beef hash braised inside tender, juicy cabbage leaves. Cabbage is also a lovely container for smoked salmon.

Wrapping salads is an inventive way of serving them. Niçoise Salad in Butter Lettuce Leaves (page 180), Romaine Leaves Stuffed with Cobb Salad (page 185), and Caesar Salad (page 182) can all be picked up, pleasing everyone who likes to eat with his or her hands.

Don't forget tamales. Corn husks and banana leaves make idea wrappers for fruited sticky rice, spicy braised pork, coconut-scented fish, even desserts. Coco-Cocoa

Tamales (page 168), for example, are a satisfying mixture of coconut, chocolate, and moist masa served with a soothing warm vanilla sauce.

Besides leaves, which are obvious wrappers because of their shape, many vegetables are suitable to a host of fillings. Eggplant, for example, is delicious wrapped around soft goat cheese and roasted red peppers.

You can also turn potatoes into interesting wraps. Stuff potato pancakes with spicy chili, curried vegetables, or melted cheddar cheese and scallions. Or form thin chips into crisp cones waiting to be filled with sour cream and chives, bits of smoked ham and herbed cream cheese, or sashimi-grade raw tuna and wasabi. These are some of our favorite stuffed vegetable recipes. We hope they will inspire you to experiment with variations of your own.

Tamales

Fresh green corn husks make excellent wrappers, but tamales are more often made of dried corn husks, which are available year-round in the Mexican section of many grocery stores.

Fresh banana leaves are also traditional tamale wrappers, particularly in the Yucatan region of Mexico and Central America. Although they are difficult to obtain north of El Paso, many Asian markets carry them frozen. Asian markets also carry ti or taro leaves and other natural wrappers. Chard, beet greens, and even cabbage leaves make good wrappers for tamales without obscuring their Mexican character.

Dried corn husks need soaking, and other wrappers may need a brief steaming to soften them before use. Look for larger husks (as wide as they are long)—these are ideal—but smaller pieces can be overlapped. Any wrapper used should be about 6 to 7 inches square, with thin strips made from extra pieces for tying the stuffed bundles.

There are three basic ways to stuff the masa with the filling. The first is to press the meat or vegetable filling into the lump of masa with a spoon or thumb. The second is to sandwich the filling between two masa patties. Some people prefer the third method of patting out a thick 3- to 4-inch patty and spreading the filling on top. It will fold over on itself as the tamale is rolled.

The easiest way to prepare masa or dough for tamales is to use masa harina (literally "dough flour") and mix it with water or other liquid. Shortening, a little baking powder, or herbs and spices can be whipped into the dough.

You can also flavor the masa with dried tomatoes, black beans, roasted garlic, or peppers. Another option is to replace the water with more flavorful liquids such as chicken or vegetable stock, the cooking liquid from pollo verde, or the water from cooking beans or other vegetables.

Basic Tamale Masa from Masa Harina

Makes enough masa for 24 to 36 tamales

$^1/2$ to 1 cup lard or shortening (optional)

4 cups masa harina

2 teaspoons salt

1 teaspoon baking powder

3 to 4 cups lukewarm water, bean cooking liquid, or chicken stock

Note When adding any food to flavor and color the masa, combine the addition with the masa harina before adding the water or stock. Use up to 4 tablespoons of chile powder or spice/herb mixes, and up to 1$^1/2$ cups of chopped or pureed vegetables. You may need to add more masa harina to balance the moisture and achieve the proper texture.

In a large mixing bowl, beat the lard with a fork or electric mixer until light and fluffy. Beat in the masa harina, salt, and baking powder. Gradually stir in the water to form a moist, soft dough. (Masa made with lard will have the consistency of perfect mashed potatoes. Made without lard, it will have a consistency similar to biscuits.) Let the masa stand for 15 minutes and adjust the moisture if needed. Use immediately or wrap tightly with plastic wrap and refrigerate up to 1 day.

Tips on Steaming Tamales

To prepare the corn husks, count out the number of pieces (plus a few extra) you'll need for your project. Place these in a deep bowl or pan or stand them up in a pitcher and cover them with warm water. Soak them until they become soft and pliable, at least 30 minutes or up to 12 hours.

To cook the tamales, use any steamer available or improvise as needed. In ancient Mexico, sticks would be placed in a clay pot to make a crude platform above a couple inches of water. Today a wire rack can be used, or if you don't have a rack, a handful of silverware can take its place. The platform needs to be just above the water, and there must be at least 2 inches of water to keep a steaming simmer going for an hour or so. Inexpensive bamboo steamers, found in Asian markets, are preferred if you are steaming a limited number of tamales. There are metal steamer baskets that fit inside most large pots. Wire racks for 13×9-inch pans (which can be sealed with foil and put in a 400°F oven) make it possible to steam dozens of tamales at once.

Many tamale cooks insist on lining the steamer with corn husks as well as covering the top with them. If the steamer is deep enough, steam them standing up with the open end on the top, being careful not to crowd them. They can be stacked, but halfway through the cooking check for cold spots (and water level) and rearrange the tamales to ensure even cooking, if necessary.

Classic Pork Tamales

Makes 24 to 36 tamales

This is also a great filling
recipe for burritos and tacos.

2 1/2 pounds boneless pork butt, shoulder,
    or loin, cut into 2- to 3-inch pieces

2 1/2 quarts water

1 head of garlic, unpeeled, cut in half
    crosswise

8 whole peppercorns

2 to 3 tablespoons vegetable oil

1 large onion, roughly chopped

6 to 9 dried ancho or New Mexico chiles,
    crushed (or 4 to 6 tablespoons New
    Mexico chile powder)

1 teaspoon chopped fresh oregano
    or 1/2 teaspoon dried

1/2 teaspoon ground cumin

Pinch of ground cloves

Pinch of ground cinnamon

1 teaspoon salt, or to taste

1/2 pound dried corn husks, soaked
    overnight

2 pounds prepared masa (page 162)

In a large pot, bring the pork and water to a boil. Skim off any foam that floats to the surface, and reduce the heat to a simmer. Add the garlic and peppercorns and cook for about 45 minutes, or until the pork is tender. Remove the mixture from the heat, let it cool slightly, and drain it, reserving the broth and meat and discarding the garlic and the peppercorns. When cool enough to handle, shred the meat into a large bowl.

In a frying pan or large saucepan, heat the oil over high heat. Add the onion and sauté it for 5 minutes, or until translucent. Stir in the chiles and cook for 30 to 45 seconds. Stir in 1 cup of the reserved broth (the remainder can be used to make masa) and the oregano, cumin, cloves, cinnamon, and salt. Turn down the heat and simmer the mixture for 5 minutes, or until the chiles are softened. Transfer the mixture to a blender or food processor and process until the mixture is smooth. Stir the mixture into the shredded meat and let it cool.

Shake the excess moisture off one of the corn husks and lay it on a flat surface. Overlap 2 smaller pieces if needed to make wrapper at least 6 inches wide. Spoon 1 to 2 tablespoons of masa in the center of the husk and flatten the masa slightly. Press 1 to 3 teaspoons of meat mixture into the center of the masa. For larger tamales, press 1 more tablespoon of masa over the mixture. Fold the left edge of the husk over the masa, then fold the right edge over. Fold the tapered bottom end of the husk up. The top or wider end can be folded down or left open, as desired. Tie a thin strip of husk around the middle of the bundle to secure it. Alternately, you can fold both the right and left sides of the husk over the filling, enclosing it completely, and then tie both ends tightly with a thin strip of husk, producing a tamale that resembles a children's party favor.

Repeat, using the remaining masa and filling. Steam the tamales for 45 minutes to $1^1/2$ hours, or until the masa is firm and the husk pulls away easily. (For tips on steaming, turn to page 163.) To serve, untie the bundles and serve with your favorite salsa. Unlike many of the wraps in this book, the actual wrap is not eaten, but keeping it on makes a nice presentation.

Yucatan Chicken Bundles

Makes 6 servings

Banana leaves are the ideal wrapper for these tamales. Although they are not edible, they impart a distinctive grassy flavor to the masa and make a pretty presentation. To soften banana leaves before folding, place cut pieces in a steamer or in boiling water for about 30 seconds, until they become pliable. Mexican cooks often soften banana leaves by heating them on a hot comal, a flat metal cooking surface used for making tortillas. A few quick turns over a stove flame will work too. You can find banana leaves as well as the seasonings in Mexican markets or the Mexican section of large supermarkets.

This savory filling is also delicious in tamales or tacos.

1 tablespoon achiote seeds or paste

1 teaspoon black peppercorns

1/2 teaspoon salt

1 tablespoon New Mexico or California chile powder

2 tablespoons olive oil

1 onion, roughly chopped

3 cloves garlic, chopped

1 tablespoon grated zest of 1 Seville orange, blood orange, or tangerine

1/3 cup fresh orange or tangerine juice

1 russet potato, peeled and shredded on a medium grater

3 boneless, skinless chicken breasts halves, thinly sliced crosswise, or 1 pound ground chicken or turkey

6 pieces (8 inches square) and 6 strips (8 × 1/4 inches) banana leaf

In an electric spice grinder or with a mortar and pestle, finely grind the achiote seeds and peppercorns. In a small bowl, combine them with the salt and chile powder and set the mixture aside.

In a large nonreactive frying pan, heat the oil over medium-high heat. Add the onion and cook for 5 minutes, stirring occasionally, until it becomes translucent. Stir in the garlic and cook for 1 minute. Stir in the achiote mix, cook for 20 seconds, and reduce the heat to medium. Stir in the zest and juice and remove the pan from the heat. Stir in the potato and let the mixture cool slightly. Stir in the chicken.

Place a banana leaf on a clean work surface with the leaf grain running up and down (perpendicular to the edge of the work surface). Place about 1/2 cup of the mixture in the center of the leaf. Fold the left and right edges of the leaf to the center so that they slightly overlap, then fold the top and bottom edges of the leaf to the center as though you were wrapping a present. Use a strip to tie the bundle. Repeat with the remaining banana leaves and filling. Steam the bundles, keeping the folds facing down, for about 30 minutes, or until firm. (Steaming tips are on page 163.) Let them cool slightly before serving. To serve, place the bundles on serving plates and let guests unwrap their own.

Steamed Fish with Coconut

1 1/2 pounds boneless firm white fish,
    such as sea bass or halibut, cut into
    1-inch cubes

3/4 cup unsweetened coconut milk

6-inch piece of lemongrass, thinly sliced
    diagonally

2 large shallots, minced (about 1/4 cup)

1 tablespoon fish sauce (Vietnamese nuoc
    cham or Thai nam pla), if available,
    or salt to taste

Grated zest of 1 lime

Grated zest of 1 orange or tangerine

Juice of 1/2 lime

6 pieces (8 inches square) and 6 strips
    (8 × 1/4 inches) banana leaf

6 sprigs cilantro (optional)

Makes 6 servings

This Southeast
Asian–inspired recipe is
easy to prepare and delicious.
Serve it with rice or steamed
potatoes to soak up the
delectable cooking juices.

In a bowl, toss the fish with the coconut milk, lemongrass, shallots, fish sauce, lime zest, orange zest, and lime juice. Let stand about 15 minutes.

See instructions for softening banana leaves in Yucatan Chicken Bundles recipe on page 166.

Place a banana leaf on a clean work surface with the leaf grain running up and down (perpendicular to the edge of the work surface). Place about 1/2 cup of the fish mixture in the center of the leaf. Top with a cilantro leaf, if desired. Fold the left and right edges of the leaf to the center so that they slightly overlap, then fold the top and bottom edges of the leaf to the center as though you were wrapping a present. Use a strip to tie the bundle. Repeat with the remaining banana leaves and filling. Steam the bundles, keeping the folds facing down, for about 15 minutes, or until firm. (Steaming tips are on page 163.) To serve, place the hot bundles on serving plates and let guests unwrap their own.

Coco-Cocoa Tamales

Makes 12 tamales

Although we're most
familiar with savory tamales,
sweet dessert versions are
popular in Mexico, especially
during the Christmas
holidays. Piloncillo is raw,
caramelized sugar that's
formed into small cone
shapes. You'll find it in
Mexican markets.

2 cups milk

2 vanilla beans or 1 tablespoon vanilla
extract

1/2 cup grated piloncillo or firmly packed
brown sugar

3/4 cup cooked rice

2/3 cup unsweetened shredded coconut

1 pound prepared masa (if you make your
own masa, use only 1/2 teaspoon salt)

2/3 cup sugar or honey

1/3 cup cocoa powder

12 pieces (6 to 7 inches square) banana
leaf or 12 moistened corn husks

12 leaf or husk strips

In a small saucepan, heat the milk, vanilla beans (if using extract, add it later), and piloncillo until the mixture reaches a simmer. As soon as it simmers, remove it from the heat, let it cool slightly, and remove and save the vanilla beans. Stir in the rice and coconut and then remove the mixture to a fine sieve. Gently press the mixture in the sieve, reserving both the liquid and the rice mixture.

See instructions for softening banana leaves in Yucatan Chicken Bundles recipe on page 166.

In a bowl, combine the masa, sugar, and cocoa and stir until thoroughly combined. Divide the mixture into 12 equal pieces. Flatten each piece into an oval about 4 inches long and 2 inches wide. Place a banana leaf on a clean work surface with the leaf grain running up and down (perpendicular to the edge of the work surface). Place the masa in the center of a banana leaf. Press about 2 tablespoons of the coconut-rice mixture into the center of the masa.

Fold the left and right edges of the leaf to the center so that they enclose the filling and slightly overlap in the center. Then fold the top and bottom edges of the leaf to the center as though you were wrapping a present. Use a strip to tie the bundle. Repeat with the remaining banana leaves and filling. Steam the bundles, keeping the folds facing down, for 30 to 45 minutes, or until firm. (Steaming tips are on page 163.)

To serve: With a sharp knife, slit open the vanilla beans and scrape the insides into the reserved milk mixture. Pour the mixture into a saucepan, add the vanilla bean husks or vanilla extract, and bring the milk to a simmer, then remove from the heat. Unwrap the tamales and place them in serving dishes. Spoon the warmed milk over each tamale.

Banana Leaves Stuffed with Fruited Rice

1 cup short-grain rice

1 cup water

2/3 cup milk

3/4 cup diced dried fruit (apricots, cranberries, papaya, or a combination)

1/2 cup sugar or honey

1/2 teaspoon aniseed

1 apple or pear, peeled, cored, and cut into 1/4-inch dice

6 pieces (8 inches square) and 6 strips (8 × 1/4 inches) banana leaf

Makes 6 servings

This unusual dessert is also great made with with Mandarin orange or tangerine segments instead of the chopped apple.

In a saucepan, bring the rice and water to a boil. Reduce the heat to a simmer, cover, and cook for 5 minutes. Stir in the milk, dried fruit, sugar, and aniseed. Simmer for about 7 minutes, until the rice is al dente but the mixture is still soupy. Stir in the apple, remove the pan from the heat, and let it cool slightly.

See instructions for softening banana leaves in Yucatan Chicken Bundles recipe on page 166.

Place a banana leaf on a clean work surface with the leaf grain running up and down (perpendicular to the edge of the work surface). Place about 1/3 cup of the rice mixture in the center of the leaf. Fold the left and right edges of the leaf to the center so that they slightly overlap, then fold the top and bottom edges of the leaf to the center as though you were wrapping a present. Use a strip to tie the bundle. Repeat with the remaining banana leaves and filling.

Place the bundles in a steamer, folded side down, and steam the wraps over simmering water for about 30 minutes, or until firm. (Steaming tips are on page 163.) Let them cool slightly before serving. Serve warm or at room temperature.

Corned Beef and Cabbage Rolls

**Makes 14 stuffed cabbage rolls,
6 to 8 servings**

A novel way to use leftovers from a traditional New England boiled dinner, this recipe features potato, onion, and corned beef hash wrapped with cabbage leaves and braised. It's a wonderful entrée or side dish for a Saint Patrick's Day buffet.

1 head of green cabbage (about 3 pounds), preferably Savoy

10 ounces cooked corned beef brisket, half shredded, half cut into 1/2-inch cubes

3 large red-skinned potatoes, diced (about 2 cups) and boiled until tender

1 carrot, diced and boiled until tender

1 small onion, minced

1 tablespoon Dijon mustard

1 tablespoon caraway seeds

2 to 3 teaspoons kosher salt (amount will depend on saltiness of the corned beef)

1 teaspoon freshly ground black pepper

3 tablespoons canola oil

About 1 cup chicken stock

Hot and sweet mustard, for garnish

Bring a large pot of water to a boil. Remove and discard any discolored outer leaves from the whole raw cabbage. With a paring knife, remove the core from the heart of the cabbage. Using 2 slotted spoons, carefully lower the whole cabbage into the boiling water. As the outermost leaves come loose, remove them with tongs and transfer them to a colander. Continue until you have removed 14 leaves. Set the cabbage leaves aside. Remove the remaining inner cabbage from the boiling water. When cool enough to handle, chop the cabbage. You'll need about 2 cups of cabbage for the filling.

In a large mixing bowl, mix together the shredded corned beef, diced corned beef, potatoes, chopped cooked cabbage, carrot, and onion. In a small bowl, combine the mustard, caraway seeds, salt, and pepper. Add the mustard mixture to the corned beef mixture and mix well.

Place a large skillet over medium-high heat. When the pan is hot, add 1 tablespoon of the oil. When the oil is hot, pack the corned beef hash mixture into the pan, forming a disk covering the surface. Fry, undisturbed, until the hash is golden brown on the bottom, about 8 to 10 minutes. Using a spatula, turn the hash to cook it on the other side. Drizzle 1 tablespoon of the oil down the sides of the skillet. Fry for 8 to 10 minutes more, then break up the hash with the spatula, drizzle the remaining 1 tablespoon of oil down the sides of the skillet and turn the broken-up pieces of hash over to brown the other side. Fry the hash for about 10 more minutes, until it is hot and crusty. Taste and adjust the seasonings if necessary. Set the cooked hash aside.

Preheat the oven to 375°F. Line up the 14 blanched cabbage leaves, core side nearest you, with the inside of each leaf facing up. Make a sharp "V" cut to remove the tough bottom part of the cabbage core from each leaf. Divide the fried corned beef hash equally among the cabbage leaves (use a scant $1/3$ cup hash per leaf), placing the hash in the center of the lower third of each leaf. Fold the core end up and over the hash. Fold the 2 sides toward the center and over the hash. Roll the covered hash away from you until you have a bundle of hash completely wrapped in cabbage. Repeat with the remaining ingredients and arrange the cabbage rolls, seam side down, in a 13×9-inch baking dish. Pour enough chicken stock over the cabbage rolls to come up $1/2$ inch from the bottom of the baking dish. Cover the dish and bake for 30 minutes. Uncover the dish and continue baking for another 10 minutes.

Remove the baking dish from the oven and let it stand for 5 minutes. Place the cabbage rolls on serving plates or a platter. Whisk 1 tablespoon of the mustard into the pan juices and drizzle the sauce over the cabbage rolls. Serve immediately with additional mustard on the side.

Note Store leftover Corned Beef and Cabbage Rolls in the refrigerator for up to 2 days. If the liquid in them has been completely absorbed and the rolls seem dry, add a little chicken stock before reheating them. Cover when reheating.

Garlic Chicken Cabbage Rolls

Makes 14 stuffed cabbage rolls,
6 to 8 servings

This recipe transforms several rather ordinary ingredients, including cabbage and the ubiquitous chicken breast, into an entrée that's definitely greater than the sum of its parts. You'll be surprised by the moistness of the chicken breasts after they're marinated and then braised with garlicky cabbage.

For a complete dinner, serve this with mashed potatoes. Or on a cold winter night, try serving 2 cabbage rolls in a soup dish with an inch of hot broth enriched with diced cooked carrots and tiny pasta such as alphabets or pastina. Garnish with minced scalliion. A loaf of hot Italian bread and a wedge of Reggiano-Parmigiano cheese complete the menu nicely.

4 cloves garlic
$1/3$ cup extra virgin olive oil
$1^1/4$ teaspoons kosher salt
$1/4$ teaspoon crushed red pepper flakes
2 boneless, skinless whole chicken breasts (about $1^1/2$ pounds)

$1^1/2$ heads of green cabbage (about 4 pounds)
1 cup chicken stock, homemade or low-sodium canned broth
1 small carrot, shredded (about $1/2$ cup)

Make the marinade: Peel the garlic and gently flatten each clove with the flat edge of a chef's knife, keeping the clove intact, if possible. In a bowl, place the garlic, oil, $1/4$ teaspoon of the salt, and half of the crushed red pepper flakes and mix until thoroughly combined.

Cut the chicken breasts across the grain into 1-inch-wide strips. Stir the chicken into the marinade. Cover the bowl, and refrigerate it at least 1 hour or up to 12 hours, if desired, stirring occasionally.

Bring a large pot of water to a boil. With a paring knife, cut out the core from the whole head of cabbage and cut away whatever core remains in the half cabbage head. Using 2 slotted spoons, carefully lower the head of cabbage into the boiling water. As the outermost leaves come loose, remove them with tongs and transfer them to a colander. Continue until you have removed 14 leaves. Set them aside.

Remove the remaining cabbage from the boiling water and let it drain in the colander. Place the half cabbage head in the water and simmer about 5 minutes until softened. Remove from the water and drain. When cool enough to handle, coarsely chop the cabbage.

Place a wok or large frying pan over high heat. With a slotted spoon, remove the chicken to the wok, leaving the oil and garlic in the bowl. Sear the chicken over high heat, being careful not to crowd the pieces, until nicely browned. Remove and set aside. (You can also cook the chicken pieces on a stovetop grill until nicely marked.) When cool enough to handle, cut the chicken into bite-size pieces.

Pour the oil from the marinade into the hot wok and discard the garlic. Add the chopped cabbage all at once and stir-fry for 1 minute. Stir in $1/4$ cup of the chicken stock and the remaining red pepper flakes and continue to braise and deglaze the cabbage. When all of the stock has been absorbed, add $1/4$ cup more stock and the carrot and continue stir-frying until the cabbage is soft and the liquid is absorbed, about 10 minutes. Combine the cabbage and chicken pieces in a large bowl and taste for seasoning, adding more salt or crushed red pepper flakes, if desired.

Preheat the oven to 375°F. Line up the 14 blanched cabbage leaves, core side nearest you, with the inside of each leaf facing up. Make a sharp "V" cut to remove the tough bottom part of the cabbage core from each leaf. Divide the cabbage-chicken mixture equally among the cabbage leaves (use a scant $1/3$ cup mixture per leaf), placing the chicken mixture in the center of the each leaf just above the core. Fold the core end up and snugly over the chicken mixture. Fold the 2 sides toward the center and over the mixture. Roll in a cylinder away from you until you have a bundle completely wrapped in cabbage. Repeat with the remaining ingredients.

Assemble the cabbage rolls, seam side down, in a 13×9-inch baking dish. Pour the remaining $1/2$ cup stock over the cabbage rolls, cover with foil, and bake for 40 minutes. Remove the pan from the oven and let it stand for 5 minutes before serving.

Leftover cabbage rolls can be stored in the refrigerator for up to 2 days. If they seem dry when you go to use them, add a little chicken stock before reheating. Cover when reheating.

This is a great recipe to remember next time you have some leftover roast chicken. Or try using bite-size pieces of grilled chicken or turkey sausages. If using leftovers, eliminate the marinating and add 3 cloves of minced garlic when you braise the chopped cabbage.

Smoked Salmon with Cabbage Leaves

Makes 8 servings

The cooking of Alsace—
a region in northeast France
on the border of Germany—
inspired this easy appetizer.
Serve the pretty dish as a
first course with a spoonful of
the peppercorn sauce. Or, if
you like, tie each cabbage
bundle with a chive and serve
without the sauce as finger
food. A glass of crisp chilled
Alsatian wine is a nice
accompaniment.

1 head of green cabbage
16 thin slices smoked salmon

PINK PEPPERCORN BEURRE BLANC
1/2 cup dry white wine
2 large shallots, peeled and finely chopped
   (about 1/4 cup)

1 cup (2 sticks) cold butter, cut into 1/2-inch
   pieces
2 tablespoons pink or green peppercorns

Bring a large pot of water to a boil. Cut out the core from the head of
cabbage. Carefully lower the head of cabbage into the water using 2 slotted
spoons. As the outermost leaves come loose, remove them with tongs and transfer them to a colander. Continue until you have removed 8 leaves. Remove the
rest of the cabbage from the boiling water and set aside to use in other recipes.

Preheat the oven to 375°F. Place a blanched cabbage leaf on a flat work
surface with the inside of the leaf facing up. Make a sharp "V" cut to remove the
tough bottom part of the cabbage core from the leaf. Cut the leaf in half. Fold a
piece of smoked salmon in half and place it in the middle of the piece of cabbage. Fold the left and right sides of the cabbage leaf over the salmon. Then roll
up the leaf from the side nearest you to completely enclose the salmon. Place
the wrap, seam side down, on a baking sheet. Repeat to wrap the remaining
salmon in the cabbage leaves. Bake the salmon for 8 to 10 minutes, or until it
is firm.

While the salmon is baking, prepare the sauce: Place the wine and shallots in a small nonreactive saucepan. Bring the mixture to a boil and cook until
the wine is reduced to about 1/4 cup. Reduce the heat to low and add the cold
butter, a piece at a time, whisking continuously until it is thoroughly incorporated and the sauce thickens. Remove the pan from the heat and stir in the pink
peppercorns.

Lightly brown the cabbage, if desired, by turning the oven to broil and
broiling the cabbage-wrapped salmon close to the source of heat for about
2 minutes.

To serve: Place a spoonful of sauce on each plate and top with 2 smoked
salmon bundles. Serve immediately.

Eggplant, Roasted Red Pepper, and Goat Cheese Roulade

1 large eggplant (about 5 inches
    in diameter)

Extra virgin olive oil

Salt to taste

Freshly ground black pepper
    to taste

1 large red bell pepper or 1 jar (8 ounces)
    roasted red peppers

1 clove garlic, finely minced

4 ounces young chèvre cheese

1 small bunch basil, thick stems removed,
    leaves cut into chiffonade

Makes 6 to 8 appetizer servings

Roasted peppers lend a tantalizing smoky taste to this flavorful dish.

It is not red pepper overkill to drizzle Red Pepper Vinaigrette (recipe follows) over this pretty appetizer or first course. Any leftover vinaigrette is delicious served with other vegetables, pasta, and fresh green salads.

Preheat the oven to 350°F. Slice the eggplant in 1/4-inch rounds. Place the eggplant slices in a single layer on an oiled baking sheet. Brush the slices with olive oil and sprinkle them with salt and pepper. Bake until tender but not mushy, about 20 minutes. Remove the eggplant slices from the oven and set them aside to cool. (You can also grill the eggplant slices, if you prefer.)

To roast the bell pepper, see instructions for roasting chiles and tomatoes in the Pollo Verde recipe on page 143.

In a small bowl, mash the garlic into the chèvre, along with salt and pepper to taste, until thoroughly combined. More garlic may be used, although the flavor intensifies as it sits.

Spread each of the eggplant slices with a thin layer of chèvre, leaving a 1/4-inch border on all sides. Top the chèvre with a slice of red pepper cut slightly smaller than the eggplant. Lightly salt and pepper the slice. Arrange basil leaves on top of the pepper. Roll the eggplant up gently but firmly, forming the roulade. Repeat with the remaining ingredients. Arrange the eggplant rolls on serving plates and garnish them with a few strips of red pepper. Drizzle with a bit more olive oil or Red Pepper Vinaigrette. Chill before serving.

Red Pepper Vinaigrette

Makes about 1 cup vinaigrette

1 roasted red bell pepper (page 143)

2 tablespoons balsamic vinegar

1 clove garlic, minced

1/3 cup olive oil

2 tablespoons water

1/2 teaspoon salt

Combine all the ingredients in a food processor and process until the mixture is smooth. Drizzle on top of roulades.

Dolmas Stuffed with Bulgur and Roasted Garlic

Makes about 60 dolmas

Traditionally, grape leaves are stuffed with rice or mixtures of rice and ground meat. In this delicious variation, the savory filling is based on nutty bulgur flavored with roasted garlic, Gorgonzola, dried fruit, and walnuts.

Grape leaves are sold in jars packaged with brine and only need to be rinsed before use. If you live near a vineyard, you can use fresh leaves that haven't been sprayed. Blanch or steam fresh leaves until they begin to wilt before using them.

4 to 6 whole heads of garlic
3/4 cup bulgur
1 cup hot water
1/2 cup golden raisins
1/2 cup chopped dried apricots
1 cup fruity white wine or apple juice
8 ounces Gorgonzola or blue cheese
2/3 cup coarsely chopped walnuts
2 teaspoons freshly ground black pepper
2 teaspoons crumbled dried sage
1 teaspoon salt
2 jars (8 ounces each) grape leaves
2 1/2 tablespoons olive oil

Preheat the oven to 300°F. Peel away the loose skin from the garlic, leaving the heads intact. Place the garlic in a baking pan, cover with aluminum foil, and bake on the bottom shelf of the oven for about 1 hour, or until the garlic softens. Let the garlic cool, then squeeze the garlic cloves from their skins into a large bowl. Add the bulgur, water, raisins, and apricots and let the mixture cool. Stir in the wine, Gorgonzola, walnuts, pepper, sage, and salt.

Preheat the oven to 375°F. Rinse the grape leaves in cold water and drain. To stuff the leaves, place a few at a time on a flat work surface with the stem end toward you and the smooth side down. Snip off any stem that might still be attached to the leaf. Spoon about 2 teaspoons of the bulgur filling along the bottom edge of the leaf. Fold the sides over the filling to the center. Then roll the leaf tightly from the stem end toward the tip, forming a neat package.

Lightly oil a 13×9-inch baking dish. Arrange the stuffed grape leaves side by side with the seam sides down in the bottom of the dish. Then form a second layer with the grape leaves perpendicular to the first layer. Add about 1 inch of water to the pan. Drizzle the grape leaves with the oil. Top with a thin layer of unfilled grape leaves. Tightly cover the dish with foil. Bake for about 40 minutes, until the dolmas are firm. Remove the pan from the oven, uncover, and let it stand about 15 minutes before serving.

Remove the dolmas from the pan with a slotted spoon and serve warm, at room temperature, or cold.

Herb-Stuffed Turkey Dolmas

1 pound ground turkey
1 cup cooked short-grain rice
1 bunch scallions, thinly sliced
    (about 1 cup)
1 large Granny Smith or Pippin apple,
    peeled, cored, and coarsely chopped
1/2 cup dry white wine or apple juice

1/4 cup chopped fresh parsley
2 tablespoons chopped fresh mint
1 teaspoon salt
2 jars (8 ounces each) grape leaves
Juice of 2 lemons
3 tablespoons extra virgin olive oil

Makes about 60 dolmas

This stuffing follows a
more traditional style but uses
lean ground turkey instead of
lamb or beef.

In a medium bowl, lightly mix together the turkey, rice, scallions, apple, wine, parsley, mint, and salt.

Preheat the oven to 375°F. Rinse the grape leaves in cold water and drain. To stuff the leaves, place a few at a time on a flat work surface with the stem end toward you and the smooth side down. Snip off any stem that might still be attached to the leaf. Spoon about 2 teaspoons of the turkey mixture along the bottom edge of each leaf. Fold the sides of the leaf over the filling to overlap in the center. Then roll the leaf tightly from the stem end toward the tip, forming a neat package.

Lightly oil a 13×9-inch baking dish. Arrange the stuffed grape leaves side by side with the seam side down in the bottom of the dish. Then form a second layer with the grape leaves perpendicular to the first layer. Add about 1 inch of water to pan. Drizzle the grape leaves with the lemon juice and olive oil. Top with a thin layer of unfilled grape leaves. Tightly cover the dish with foil. Bake for about 40 minutes, until the dolmas are firm. Remove the pan from the oven, uncover, and let stand for about 15 minutes before serving.

Remove the dolmas with a slotted spoon and serve them warm, at room temperature, or cold. Sprinkle with additional lemon juice, if desired.

Mustard Greens Filled with Jambalaya

Makes 6 servings, 2 bundles per person

Use tender young mustard greens, if you can find them, although more mature greens will work too. If you use older greens, you will have to cook them slightly longer. It's a good idea to cook a few extra leaves in case any tear and you need to patch them.

2 tablespoons canola oil

1/2 onion, cut into 1/2-inch cubes

1 stalk celery, cut into 1/2-inch cubes

1/2 green bell pepper, cut into 1/2-inch squares

3/4 cup long-grain white rice

1 cup fish stock or clam juice

1 1/2 cups chicken stock

2 ripe tomatoes, peeled, seeded, and diced, or 1 cup chopped canned tomatoes

1 pound boneless, skinless chicken thighs, cut into 1/2-inch cubes (6 to 7 chicken thighs)

3 cloves garlic, minced

1 tablespoon paprika

1 bay leaf

2 teaspoons freshly ground black pepper

2 1/2 teaspoons gumbo filé

1 teaspoon dried thyme

1/4 teaspoon cayenne pepper

1/2 pound tasso or smoked ham, cut into 1/2-inch cubes

1/2 pound smoked sausage, thinly sliced

Salt to taste

24 young mustard green leaves or 12 larger leaves (about 6 inches wide at the widest part)

In a large saucepan, heat the oil over medium heat. Add the onion, celery, and bell pepper and cook, stirring occasionally, until the onion becomes translucent, about 8 minutes.

Stir in the rice, fish stock, 1 cup of the chicken stock, tomatoes, chicken pieces, garlic, paprika, bay leaf, black pepper, filé, thyme, and cayenne. Bring the mixture to a simmer. Cover, reduce the heat to a low simmer, and cook for 15 to 20 minutes, until the rice is tender.

Add the tasso and sausage. Cover and cook 10 minutes longer. Remove the pan from the heat and let cool.

Bring a large pot of salted water to a boil. Fill a large bowl with ice water. Add the mustard greens to the boiling water in 2 batches, gently pushing the leaves under the water so they wilt and cook. (Young leaves need only to be blanched. Larger, more mature leaves will need to cook 2 to 3 minutes.) When the mustard greens are wilted, carefully remove them with a wide Chinese mesh spoon (or a flat strainer—tongs might tear the leaves), and immediately place them in the bowl of ice water to prevent further cooking. When the leaves are cool, carefully remove them from the water and spread them out flat on paper towels. Keep them covered with a damp kitchen towel. Stuff them immediately or refrigerate them overnight and stuff them the next day.

To assemble: On a flat work surface, criss-cross 2 young mustard green leaves. Place $1/2$ cup jambalaya in the center of the leaves. Bring the leaves up and fold them over the filling, making a fat, roundish package. Arrange the stuffed mustard green leaves, seam side down, in a 13×9-inch baking dish. (If you're using larger leaves, use a paring knife to cut along and around the stem to remove it. Overlap the leaf "flaps" to form a whole leaf.)

Preheat the oven to 350°F. Pour the remaining $1/2$ cup chicken stock over the wraps to moisten the mustard greens. Cover the pan tightly with aluminum foil and bake for about 15 minutes to heat through. Be careful when lifting the foil, as steam will escape.

Niçoise Salad in Butter Lettuce Wrappers

Makes 8 to 12 hand-held salads, depending on size of lettuce leaves; serves 4 to 6 as a salad course or 3 to 4 as a lunch entrée

This salad is especially flavorful when made with grilled fresh albacore and garden tomatoes.

You can also use the crisp outer leaves of iceberg lettuce instead of the more delicate butter variety. Pack the salad mixture lengthwise along one edge of an iceberg lettuce leaf and roll the stuffed leaf into a cylindrical shape. If you use iceberg lettuce, wrap each salad tightly in plastic wrap and refrigerate for up to 3 hours. Unwrap the plastic wrap as you eat the portable salad, keeping the bottom of the plastic wrap in place to catch any drips.

2 teaspoons extra virgin olive oil

10 ounces fresh albacore tuna steaks, cut 1 inch thick, or 2 cans (6 ounces each) fancy albacore solid white tuna, drained and flaked

Freshly ground black pepper to taste

2 medium red potatoes (about 8 ounces total)

1 tin (2 ounces) anchovies packed in olive oil, drained

1 teaspoon minced garlic

3/4 teaspoon dry mustard

1 to 2 tablespoons fresh lemon juice

1/2 cup mayonnaise

3/4 teaspoon champagne vinegar or cider vinegar

1/2 pound fresh green beans, trimmed and cut into 1/2-inch lengths

Kosher salt to taste

1 small red onion, finely diced

2 large eggs, hard-boiled, chopped into 1/2-inch pieces

1 jar (6 1/2 ounces) marinated artichoke hearts, drained and chopped into 1/2-inch pieces (optional)

1/2 cup pitted and roughly chopped Niçoise olives

2 ripe tomatoes (about 1/2 pound), cut into 1/2-inch cubes, or 1/2 pound cherry tomatoes, cut in half

1 tablespoon capers, rinsed and drained

1 large head of butter lettuce, leaves separated, washed, and dried

Brush the olive oil onto both sides and all around the edges of the tuna. Season with pepper and set aside. Or toss the canned tuna with the olive oil and add salt and pepper to taste before adding the tuna to the dressing.

Place the potatoes in a saucepan with enough water to cover them. Bring the water to a boil, reduce the heat, and simmer the potatoes until they are tender, about 20 minutes.

Prepare the dressing: In a large mixing bowl, mash together the anchovies, garlic, dry mustard, and lemon juice using a fork. Whisk in the mayonnaise.

When the potatoes are cooked, transfer them to a shallow mixing bowl. While still warm but cool enough to handle, cut the potatoes into 1/2-inch cubes and sprinkle them with the vinegar. Toss to coat evenly and transfer the potatoes to the bowl containing the dressing. Mix lightly, just to combine.

Steam the green beans until crisp-tender, about 3 minutes. Add the hot green beans to the potatoes and mix lightly. Set the mixture aside.

Light a charcoal grill or preheat a gas grill or broiler. Grill or broil the tuna for 3 minutes. Turn the fish over and grill for another 2 minutes, or to the desired doneness. Transfer the cooked fish to a plate and season both sides with salt. Set the fish aside to cool. When it has cooled, use a fork to flake it into 1/2-inch chunks.

Add the fish, onion, hard-boiled eggs, artichoke hearts, olives, 2/3 of the fresh tomatoes, and half of the capers to the bowl with the potatoes and beans. Toss together lightly. Taste for seasonings and adjust if necessary.

In a small bowl, toss the remaining capers and tomatoes together.

Arrange 8 to 12 lettuce leaves with the inside of each leaf facing up on a serving platter. Divide the salad mixture among the leaves, mounding between 1 and 4 tablespoons of salad into the center of each leaf, depending on the size of the leaf. Leave about a 3/4-inch margin around all sides of each leaf for ease in picking up and eating. Use the tomato and caper mixture to garnish each salad. Serve immediately. Eat out of hand (over a plate or napkin) by picking up a filled leaf and folding the 2 margins of lettuce over the filling.

Pick-Up Caesar Salads

Makes 8 servings

Picked up and eaten like a hot dog in a bun, this is a zesty, eggless version of the classic salad.

2 heads of romaine lettuce (about 1 pound each)

3/4 cup light-flavored olive oil

5 cloves garlic, peeled

2 cups fresh bread crumbs (see note below)

1 tin (2 ounces) anchovies packed in olive oil, drained

2 tablespoons fresh lemon juice

1 teaspoon champagne vinegar or white wine vinegar

1 1/2 teaspoons minced lemon zest

1 teaspoon salt

Freshly ground black pepper to taste

4 ounces Parmigiano-Reggiano cheese

Remove and discard any blemished outer leaves from both heads of lettuce. Break off 8 perfect outer leaves, each measuring about 5 to 6 inches across the top at the widest point and 8 to 10 inches long. Trim the bottoms of the 8 leaves.

Cut the remaining inner leaves from both heads of lettuce into 1/4-inch-wide shreds. You'll need 8 cups of tightly packed romaine pieces. Separately wash and spin-dry the 8 outer leaves and the pieces of romaine. Set aside.

Heat a frying pan over medium-low heat. When the pan is hot, reduce the heat to low and add 1/4 cup of the olive oil. Gently crush 4 of the garlic cloves with the flat side of a knife blade. When the oil is warm, add the crushed garlic. Swirl the garlic around in the oil, turning it often and being careful not to let it brown. When it just begins to take on color, adjust the heat to medium-high and add the bread crumbs all at once. Stir constantly with a flat-edged spatula until the crumbs are uniformly golden brown. Transfer the sautéed garlic and bread crumbs to a large bowl lined with several paper towels. Blot the crumbs with more paper towels. Remove the sautéed garlic and place it in a food processor. (If the garlic is dark brown, discard it and use fresh garlic in its place.) Transfer 3 tablespoons of crumbs to a small bowl for garnish and set both bowls aside.

Prepare the dressing: In a food processor, combine half of the anchovies, the lemon juice, vinegar, lemon zest, salt, and pepper. Process, scraping the bowl occasionally, until all ingredients are blended. With the motor running, slowly drizzle in the remaining 1/2 cup olive oil to make a smooth, emulsified dressing. Taste for seasonings and adjust, if necessary. Set the dressing aside.

Using a vegetable peeler with a nonswivel blade (or the largest hole on the side of a box grater), pare off about 40 shards of Parmigiano-Reggiano onto a plate and set them aside. Grate the remaining cheese into a bowl, then transfer 3 tablespoons of the cheese to a small bowl for garnish and set the plate and both bowls aside.

Cut the remaining clove of garlic in half crosswise and rub the cut sides all over the inside surfaces of a large wooden salad bowl. Rub the garlic over the surface of a serving platter and cover the platter with the 8 whole leaves of romaine lettuce. Discard the garlic.

Place the romaine chiffonade in the salad bowl and toss with the dressing. Add the larger bowls of bread crumbs and grated cheese and toss well. Divide the tossed salad equally among the whole romaine leaves. Garnish each with the remaining 3 tablespoons bread crumbs, the remaining 3 tablespoons grated cheese and about 5 shards of Parmesan each. Cut the remaining anchovies into small pieces and scatter them over each salad. Serve immediately.

Note To prepare 2 cups fresh bread crumbs, remove the crusts from about 5 ounces of day-old French or Italian bread. Cut the bread into 1-inch pieces and place in a food processor, half at a time. Process until the crumbs are $1/4$ to $1/2$ inch in size, about 20 to 30 seconds. You should have about 2 cups of fresh bread crumbs. Store any extra bread crumbs in a plastic bag in the freezer for another use.

Lamb Dolmas Agrodolce

Makes about 60 dolmas

Agrodolce means "sweet and sour" in Italian. These stuffed grape leaves demonstrate the powerful influence North Africa and the Middle East have had on Sicilian food.

1/4 cup olive oil
1 large yellow onion, coarsely chopped
6 large cloves garlic, coarsely chopped
2 pounds ground lamb
1 cup dry red wine or cranberry juice
3/4 cup dried cranberries, coarsely chopped
3 tablespoons honey
2 tablespoons balsamic vinegar

Juice of 2 lemons
1 tablespoon freshly ground black pepper
1 tablespoon paprika
1 teaspoon salt
1/2 teaspoon ground cinnamon
1/2 teaspoon ground allspice
2 jars (8 ounces each) grape leaves

In a large frying pan, heat 2 tablespoons of the olive oil over high heat. Add the onion and sauté for about 5 minutes, until it becomes translucent. Stir in the garlic and sauté 2 minutes longer. Remove the pan from the heat and stir in the lamb, wine, cranberries, honey, vinegar, lemon juice, pepper, paprika, salt, cinnamon, and allspice. Let the mixture cool.

Preheat the oven to 375°F. Rinse the grape leaves in cold water and drain. To stuff the leaves, place a few at a time on a flat work surface with the stem end toward you and the smooth side down. Snip off any stem that might still be attached to the leaf. Spoon about 2 teaspoons of the lamb mixture along the bottom edge of the leaf. Fold the sides over the filling to overlap slightly in the center. Then roll the leaf tightly from the stem end toward the tip, forming a neat package.

Lightly oil a 13×9-inch baking dish. Arrange the stuffed grape leaves side by side with the seam side down in the bottom of the dish. Then form a second layer with the stuffed grape leaves perpendicular to first layer. Add about 1 inch of water to pan. Drizzle the grape leaves with the remaining 2 tablespoons of oil. Top with a thin layer of unfilled grape leaves. Tightly cover the dish with foil. Bake for about 40 minutes, until the dolmas are firm. Remove the pan from the oven, uncover, and let stand about 15 minutes before serving.

Remove the dolmas from the pan with a slotted spoon and serve them warm, at room temperature, or cold. Sprinkle with additional lemon juice, if desired.

Romaine Leaves Stuffed with Cobb Salad

8 strips bacon, cooked until crisp

4 large eggs, hard-boiled and peeled

2 heads romaine lettuce (about 1 pound each)

4 ounces roast turkey or leftover roast chicken, cut into 1/4-inch dice

4 ounces baked or smoked ham, cut into 1/4-inch dice

1 red onion, diced

1 avocado, peeled, pitted, and cut into 1/4-inch dice

2 ripe tomatoes, diced

2 ounces Maytag or other high-quality domestic blue cheese, crumbled (about 1/2 cup)

1/2 cup Cobb Salad Dressing (recipe follows)

Makes 8 stuffed romaine leaves, 4 servings

The beloved Cobb salad is as popular today as it was in 1926 when the chef of Los Angeles's Brown Derby restaurant created it in honor of his boss, owner Robert Cobb. This delicious variation features a mélange of diced meats and lettuce with bits of creamy ripe avocado, fresh tomato, bacon, and crumbled blue cheese served on crisp leaves of romaine. To eat, simply fold the leaf over the zesty filling.

Chill a serving platter large enough to hold 8 outer leaves of romaine lettuce. Cut half of the bacon into 1/4-inch pieces and crumble the remaining 4 strips. Set both aside in separate containers. Finely chop the hard-boiled eggs, cover, and set aside.

Remove and discard any blemished outside leaves from both heads of lettuce. Break off 8 outer leaves and trim the bottom of the leaves. Cut the remaining inner leaves from both heads of lettuce into 1/4-inch shreds or chiffonade. Stop when you have 2 quarts of moderately packed chiffonade. (Reserve any remaining romaine leaves for another use.) Wash and spin-dry the leaves and the chiffonade.

In a very large mixing bowl, toss together the romaine chiffonade, turkey, ham, bacon pieces, red onion, avocado, tomatoes, blue cheese, and half of the chopped eggs. Pour the salad dressing over the salad and toss lightly.

Arrange the 8 outer leaves of romaine on the chilled platter. Divide the Cobb salad equally among the romaine leaves, mounding the salad slightly in the center of each leaf. Garnish with the remaining chopped eggs and crumbled bacon. Fold the edges of the leaf around the filling and eat as finger food.

Cobb Salad Dressing

Makes 3/4 cup dressing

2 cloves garlic, peeled

2 teaspoons chopped fresh thyme

2 teaspoons sugar

1 teaspoon salt

1 teaspoon dry mustard

*2 tablespoons unseasoned rice vinegar
   or sherry vinegar*

2 tablespoons fresh orange juice

1/2 teaspoon balsamic vinegar

1/2 cup canola oil

Smash the garlic cloves with the flat side of a chef's knife. Transfer them to a blender or food processor. Add the thyme, sugar, salt, and dry mustard; blend well. Add the rice vinegar, orange juice, and balsamic vinegar and blend well. Scrape down the sides. With the machine running, slowly drizzle in the oil. Taste for seasonings and adjust, if necessary. Any leftover dressing can be kept in the refrigerator for several days and used over any green salad. It's best to taste and check the seasonings before serving.

Potato Chip Cones

1 extra-large russet potato
Oil for deep-frying

Makes about 24 cones

Using a mandoline or Japanese slicer, cut the potato on its flatter, wider surface into slices the thickness of thick potato chips, about $1/8$ inch. Place the slices in a bath of ice water as you work to prevent browning.

Heat 2 to 3 inches of oil in a deep, heavy saucepan to 360°F (a tip of a potato slice dipped in the oil will bubble vigorously). Dry the potato slices on paper towels before frying. Blanch the potato slices in the hot oil, a few slices at a time, only long enough to soften them, 30 to 45 seconds. Be sure the slices don't take on any color. Drain the slices well and allow them to cool in a single layer on paper towels.

To form cones, wrap one end of a potato slice over the other, making a cornucopia shape. Secure with a toothpick, with one end of the toothpick extending past the edge of the cone to allow for easy removal.

Fry the cones, a few at a time, until they turn golden brown, about 45 seconds. Carefully remove the cones from the oil and drain them on paper towels. When cool enough to handle, remove the toothpicks.

Fill just before serving. For firm fillings such as flavored cream cheese, use a piping bag. Most fillings can simply be spooned into the opening.

Fill these bite-size, crisp potato cones with anything that strikes your fancy, including sour cream and chives, brilliant deep-orange salmon roe or sturgeon caviar. Try crème fraîche or softened cream cheese and smoked salmon, a bit of seared foie gras and caramelized onions, chopped sashimi-grade raw tuna with wasabi and scallions or, if you win the lottery, a bit of fresh truffle. Salt or not, depending on the filling.

Potatoes for these chips may be peeled or left unpeeled for a more rustic look and earthier flavor. If you decide not to peel the potatoes, be sure to scrub them well.

To ensure that the cones stay crisp, serve shortly after filling.

Stuffed Potato Pancakes

These unusual potato pancakes conceal a tasty surprise inside. A savory filling is stuffed between 2 mashed russet or sweet potato cakes in a delicious variation of potato pancakes. What a great way to transform leftover mashed or baked potatoes into a delicious light meal!

The filling possibilities are endless. For example, stuff russet potato pancakes with any of the following:

Sautéed onion and grated zucchini with bits of roasted red pepper

Leftover lamb stew, the pieces of meat cut small, with roasted garlic and rosemary

Spicy salsa and soft cream or goat cheese

Diced cooked beets and sautéed onion garnished with sour cream and salmon roe

Shredded or diced turkey and cranberry sauce

Thick chili garnished with sour cream and salsa

Curried cauliflower, sautéed onions, and sweet peas

Season the mashed potatoes with curry and stuff them with ground lamb and onions seasoned with ground cumin. Garnish the pancakes with grated cucumber, a swirl of yogurt, and cilantro sprigs.

Fill mashed sweet potato or yam pancakes with:

Caramelized onions and chutney

Smoky-sweet baked beans and small pieces of baked ham or barbecued pork

Roast turkey, stuffing, and gravy. Garnish with cranberry sauce for Thanksgiving Day II.

Russet Potato Pancakes Stuffed with Cheddar Cheese and Scallions

2 cups cooked (baked or boiled) russet
   potatoes, peeled and cooled

1/4 cup milk

Butter to taste

Salt to taste

1 egg, beaten

Plain fresh bread crumbs (optional)

1/2 cup grated sharp cheddar cheese

1/4 cup thinly sliced scallions

Butter, oil, or nonstick pan spray

**Makes 6 to 8 pancakes,
3 to 4 servings**

Here's a specific recipe

to start your creativity

cooking.

In a large bowl, mash the potatoes with the milk and butter until they are thick and slightly lumpy. Add more milk, if necessary, but only until the potatoes form a stiff paste. The potatoes should be stiffer than regular mashed potatoes. If using leftover mashed potatoes, do not add milk. Add salt to taste. Thoroughly mix in the egg. If the potato mixture is too soft to be picked up and patted into a pancake, add just enough bread crumbs to make the mixture workable.

To make the stuffed potatoes: Form 2 pancakes at a time, each 3 inches in diameter and no more than 1/4 inch thick. Place a generous tablespoon of the cheese on top of one of the pancakes, spreading it evenly over the surface, leaving a 1/2-inch border uncovered all around. Sprinkle with a teaspoon or so of scallions and top with the other pancake. Press the edges together to form a secure seal. If the pancakes are not sticking together, the border may be brushed very lightly with beaten egg. Each pancake will measure about 3 inches wide and 5/8 inch thick. Repeat this procedure until all the ingredients are used up.

In a large, heavy frying pan, heat 2 tablespoons butter or oil over medium-high heat. (Or use pan spray or a nonstick pan with 1 teaspoon butter or oil to cut back on fat.) Add as many pancakes as will comfortably fit in a single layer—do not crowd. Brown the pancakes on one side, about 6 minutes. Then turn them over and brown the other side. Keep the finished pancakes warm in a 250°F oven while you cook the second batch. You may need to add more butter or oil to the frying pan.

Glossary

AHI TUNA   Another term for the large bluefin tuna, popular for its firm, deep red flesh and rich, buttery flavor. Ahi tuna is perfect for searing. Sushi-grade ahi tuna will be very fresh; it should have wide-grained flesh with no white striations.

ANAHEIM CHILE   A large green or red chile pepper, about 6 inches long and 2 inches wide, that is often filled and roasted.

ANNATTO SEED (or ACHIOTE)   A small, dark red seed of a small flowering tree of the tropics. Used extensively in Latin American and Southeast Asian cooking to color foods a distinctive red as well as add its subtle flavor. The very hard seeds are either fried in oil to release their color and flavor before being strained out and discarded, or else they are processed to a powder. You can also find it in a more convenient paste form that is often labeled "recado."

ASAFETIDA   Obtained from the milky resin of a Middle Eastern plant, this pungent seasoning is used throughout Indian cuisine. Redolent of onion and garlic, it is very strong; only a very small amount of the powder is needed to add savory depth to any dish.

BAIN-MARIE   A classic French utensil that is very similar to a double boiler, consisting of a small bowl or pan that fits snugly on top of another pan in which water is kept hot or gently simmered. As steam from the water rises, the contents of the upper container are warmed gently, essential for fragile ingredients such as custard sauces or chocolate. Also known as a water bath.

BALSAMIC VINEGAR   A dark, mellow, slightly sweet vinegar from Italy. Made from grapes and aged in wooden casks, the best balsamic vinegar originates from the city of Modena.

BAMBOO SHOOTS   The young, tender points of bamboo plants. Widely available sliced or whole in cans, but infinitely better are those available at Asian markets, either fresh (which must be parboiled before using) or preserved in a brine (which only need to be rinsed). They should be cream or very pale yellow colored, with a fresh woodsy scent, a sweet flavor, and a firm, crunchy texture. Store bamboo shoots covered with cold water for up to 3 days in the refrigerator.

BAMBOO STEAMER   Round lattice trays that stack up conveniently to allow large amounts of food to be steamed at once. They are large enough to be placed over a pot of boiling water for longer steaming times and are attractive enough to serve the food from them directly. Available in Asian markets and gourmet kitchen-supply stores.

BANANA LEAVES   The large, glossy, dark green leaves of banana trees, used in tropical countries throughout the world to wrap foods for steaming, boiling, and grilling. Besides keeping food moist, the leaves contribute their distinctive flavor to both savory dishes and desserts. They can be found frozen in Asian markets.

BLANCH To cook very briefly in a large amount of boiling salted water. Blanching helps loosen the peel of various fruits and vegetables, sets the color of greens, and cooks vegetables just to the point of tender-crispness. Foods are then immediately "refreshed" by quick submersion in iced water to stop the cooking.

BRAISE To cook meat or vegetables with a minimal amount of flavorful liquid in a tightly covered pan, often after the ingredients are sautéed first to sear and brown them.

BUCKWHEAT FLOUR The seed of a plant related to rhubarb that is hulled and then ground. The flour has a light purple-gray hue with darker speckles and a distinctive nutty flavor and grainy texture.

BULGUR Wheat that has been hulled, steamed, and cracked between rollers to form small granules, then dried to a pale golden color. Requiring only a short soaking in boiling water, bulgur is a versatile and healthful staple in Middle Eastern cuisines.

CAPERS The unopened flower buds of a small shrub that grows wild on high cliffs throughout the Mediterranean region. Capers are widely available in supermarkets pickled in vinegar; soak first in warm water for 10 minutes, then drain, to cut the harshness of the brine. Nonpareil designates the more desirable, smaller capers from Provence. If the buds are particularly large, chop roughly before adding to a recipe.

CHIFFONADE To finely cut a leafy green or large-leafed herb into very thin strips. After washing and drying the leaves, remove the stems. Stack a few leaves at a time, grouping similar-size leaves together for neater cutting, and roll the stack tightly to form a cylinder. With a very sharp knife, cut the roll crosswise into very thin strips 1/8 inch wide or thinner, depending on the recipe. The greens will unfurl into long strands; gently lift and loosen them before using in recipes.

CHILE OIL A bright red, very spicy flavoring oil that has been infused with hot peppers. It is not used for frying but rather is added to a dish toward the end of cooking. Available in Asian markets or in the ethnic aisle at supermarkets.

CHOP To cut vegetables, seasonings, or meat into relatively large bite-size pieces, usually not more than 1/2 inch in size. Coarsely chop refers to larger pieces and implies that less attention to exact shape is needed.

CILANTRO A leafy green herb with a distinctive lemony bite that is essential in Southeast Asian and Latin American cuisines. Cilantro is also known as Chinese parsley and is occasionally labeled coriander because its leaves come from the same plant that produces the coriander seed. The herb's flavor diminishes quickly with heat, so add as garnish just before serving or use in uncooked salads and sauces.

COCONUT MILK   The thick, rich juice drained from ripe coconuts. It is available in cans in the ethnic aisle of supermarkets, as well as in Asian markets. Mix well before using, since the cream tends to separate from the oils.

CORN HUSKS   Flattened and dried to a light beige color, corn husks are used through-out Mexico for wrapping foods, in particular, tamales. The husks lend their flavor to the foods they are steamed in. They need to be soaked in hot water until soft and pliable; reserve a few to tear into strips for tying the tamales.

CURRY POWDER   A complex blend of freshly roasted and ground spices that flavors sauces in Indian cuisine. The term, in fact, comes from an Indian word meaning "sauce." Whereas in the West, a generic yellow mix is synonymous with any curry dish, in India every recipe requires a different blend of spices, sometimes reaching almost 30 in number. Look in Indian markets for more interesting and authentic spice blends.

DAIKON RADISH   A large white, sweet, slightly peppery radish that is used throughout Asian cooking. It is braised as a vegetable, preserved as spicy pickles, or grated as a condi-ment. Daikon radishes grow over a foot in length, but choose the smaller ones for less fibrous flesh. Available in Asian markets and increasingly appearing in supermarkets.

DICE   To cut vegetables or meat into cube-shaped pieces for decorative appeal as well as even cooking. Small dice generally refers to very tiny cubes measuring about $1/8$ inch along each side. More common, however, are medium dice with $1/4$-inch sides and large dice, or cubes, with $1/2$-inch sides. (If no size is specified, then dice the ingredients into cubes just under $1/2$ inch in size.) The easiest way to dice is first to cut the vegetable into slices of the appropriate width and then to cut the slices into strips of the same thick-ness. Finally, cut the strips crosswise to make cubes.

DOLMAS   A classic of Greek or Turkish cuisines. These bite-size rolls consist of a filling of rice and ground meat flavored with dill and mint, enclosed in a wrapper of grape leaves. They can be served warm with a lemony sauce or cold marinated in olive oil and herbs.

EMPANADA   Filled with meat, vegetable, or fruit fillings, these flaky pastry turnovers are popular throughout Spain and Latin America.

FILO   Paper-thin sheets of dough used in Middle Eastern and Greek cuisines. They are brushed with butter or olive oil, layered, and then filled with either savory or sweet fillings to make delicate, airy pastries. Packages of filo (also spelled "phyllo") are widely available in the frozen food section of supermarkets; look in Middle Eastern markets for fresh sheets of filo.

FISH SAUCE   A basic seasoning in Southeast Asia made from fresh anchovies that are layered with salt and then strained to produce a thin, clear, amber-colored sauce. Used like salt, a few drops are sprinkled in nearly every dish to add depth to other flavors. It is also a condiment and an essential ingredient in many dipping sauces.

FIVE-SPICE POWDER   An aromatic mixture of ground spices used throughout China in dumpling fillings, marinades, and mixed with salt as a condiment. Based on an ancient medicinal formula, it usually contains cassia bark, cloves, fennel seed, star anise, and Sichuan peppercorns but may also include licorice root and ground ginger. Available in small bags at Asian markets and frequently in the spice section of supermarkets.

FRAMBOISE   An eau-de-vie distilled from raspberries that adds intense berry flavor to desserts and sauces.

FRESH BREAD CRUMBS   Far superior to the dry, dusty texture of prepared dry bread crumbs, fresh bread crumbs are easy to make by processing trimmed white bread slices in a blender or food processor.

GARAM MASALA   A blend of roasted, dried, and ground spices from northern India that may include cinnamon, cloves, coriander, cardamom, fennel, and dried chiles, as well as other warm spices. The formula varies with every cook, and the best are prepared just before cooking, but look for small packages in Indian markets and supermarkets.

GIANDUIA   Chocolate blended with hazelnuts for rich flavor and velvety texture. It is usually made with milk chocolate, but bittersweet and semisweet are also available. Look in gourmet markets or baking and confectionary shops for this chocolate. It has a short shelf life; store for up to 6 months in a cool, dark place.

GINGER   The golden tan, gnarled root of a tropical plant. Its faintly sweet flavor, with a peppery bite, is essential to Asian and Indian cooking. A very versatile and popular aromatic seasoning, it can grated, minced, slivered, or sliced. Look for smaller roots with smooth, shiny skin; old ginger will be dry and fibrous. If it will be eaten, the peel should be removed. Wrap in a paper towel, then store in a plastic bag in the refrigerator for up to 2 weeks.

GRAPE LEAVES   While used fresh in Greece to make dolmas and to wrap various foods before roasting and grilling, grape leaves are more commonly available preserved in a brine. Rinse well to remove as much of the salt as possible before using.

GUMBO FILE A traditional ingredient in Creole cooking. Prepared from sassafras leaves, filé is stirred into dishes at the end of cooking to thicken sauces and add a subtle root beer–like flavor. Available as a powder in the spice section of supermarkets.

HOISIN SAUCE A thick, sweet, brownish red sauce made from soybeans and flavored with five-spice powder. Used in China in glazes and as a condiment for roast pork and poultry. Look for jars of hoisin in Asian markets or in the Asian section of supermarkets.

INSTANT-READ THERMOMETER A small thermometer that quickly registers the temperature of foods when the stem is inserted in meats or submerged in liquids. Crucial for checking the doneness of roasts and gauging the temperature of water, these are available in kitchen-supply stores.

JALAPEÑO CHILE This small, squat, and slightly tapered chile pepper can be either green or red. It has medium heat and a sweet flavor that makes it very popular in salsas, dips, and as a condiment.

JASMINE RICE A long-grained, very fragrant rice that is a staple in Thailand and Vietnam. It's available in large bags in Asian markets or in small boxes in the gourmet section of supermarkets.

JICAMA A large root with thin, golden brown skin and crisp, white, sweetly flavored flesh. It can be served fresh or cooked; peel the fibrous skin just before using.

JULIENNE To cut ingredients into thin strips the shape and size of matchsticks. Generally, vegetables or cooked meat are first cut into slices about 1/8 inch, then these slices are stacked and cut crosswise again 1/8 inch thick, to form thin strips 3 to 4 inches in length.

LEMONGRASS An herb with a citrusy flavor that is important in Southeast Asian cuisine. It resembles a thin scallion in shape but has a woody texture and very pale green upper stems. Only the bottom white part of the stem is used, either puréed with other aromatic ingredients or else cut, crushed, then added to stocks to infuse soups with its tart flavor. While it is available dried, fresh lemongrass, which is much more fragrant, is readily found in supermarkets and Asian markets.

MASA Derived from the Spanish word for "dough," masa is used to make corn tortillas, tamales, and various southwestern breads. Masa harina is a fine flour made from dried corn that has been treated with lime and then ground while still wet.

MATZO An unleavened bread, resembling a large, crisp cracker, that is traditionally served and used in recipes during the Jewish Passover holiday.

MINCE To cut herbs, vegetables, or meat into very small pieces, usually less than 1/8 inch in size.

MIRIN A golden-colored, sweetened Japanese rice wine that is used exclusively for cooking to enhance sauces and glazes. A sweet sherry can be used instead.

MUNG BEAN THREAD NOODLES Thin, wiry noodles made from mung beans that are transparent and silky after cooking. They are soaked first in warm water then used in fillings, braises, stir-fries, and soups. Look for the noodles in Asian markets, in packages of 8 to 10 small skeins.

NONREACTIVE Refers to cooking and serving equipment made of Teflon, stainless steel, glass, enameled steel, or ceramic. In contrast, cookware made from aluminum will react with salt solutions and with acidic ingredients such as lemon juice, vinegar, wine, and even tomatoes, darkening the foods a shade of gray.

OYSTER SAUCE A thick, brown, richly flavored sauce made from dried oysters. It is used in China for stir-fried and braised dishes and as a condiment on steamed green vegetables.

PANCETTA An Italian bacon that is seasoned with black pepper and cured but not smoked. Pancetta is rolled into a cylindrical shape. Look for it in an Italian market, where it will be freshest.

PARCHMENT PAPER Heavy paper that is coated to resist grease. It is used extensively in baking to line pans but is also used in savory dishes, especially for steaming and cooking food in packets.

PASTRY BRUSH A small brush used for applying glazes and egg washes delicately and evenly on breads and rolls before baking.

PASTRY FLOUR Made from wheat low in gluten and high in starch. With slightly more protein than cake flour, it provides more structure while ensuring a tender, crumbly texture in baked goods.

PEPERONCINI Short, light green, relatively mild peppers that are pickled and served as a condiment or added to salads.

PINE NUTS The small, ivory-colored seed of a pine tree with a rich flavor popular in Italian and Northern Asian cuisines. Also known as pignoli.

POACH To simmer fish, vegetables, or fruits very gently in stock or salted water. The temperature ranges between 160° and 200°F, depending on the dish, but the liquid should be kept at a steady heat.

POBLANO CHILE   A wide, sharply tapering chile pepper that is dark green with a dark purple tinge. It varies in heat from medium to hot and is always used cooked. It is often roasted to bring out its smoky flavor.

PROSCIUTTO   An Italian salt-cured ham that is air-dried. It has a delicate flavor and texture that are highlighted in simple appetizers; it is also often added to pasta sauces or rolled as a filling in meats. Look in Italian or gourmet food markets, where it is best freshly cut into thin, transparent slices.

PURÉE   To blend in a food processor, food mill, or blender.

RADICCHIO   An Italian cousin of chicory that has tender red leaves loosely packed in a small head and a subtle peppery bite.

RAVIOLI   A classic of Italian cuisine, these little pillows are formed from flat sheets of pasta that are filled with meat, cheese, or vegetables and then cut into squares or rounds. They are usually boiled and served with a sauce.

RICE PAPER   Made from a rice flour batter that is spread thin and dried to brittle, transparent sheets. They are reconstituted in warm water and then used to wrap around various fillings. Look for packages in Asian markets.

RICE STICKS   Thin rice noodles used throughout Southeast Asia as the base for a wide variety of soups and stir-fried noodle dishes. Look in Asian markets for large square-shaped skeins.

RICOTTA CHEESE   A fresh white cheese with a rich, slightly sweet flavor, used in Italy for both savory and dessert dishes. Made from both whole or skim milk. Substitute with farmer's or drained small-curd cottage cheese.

SAUTÉ   To cook cut vegetables or small cuts of meat in a frying pan with a small amount of oil over high or medium-high heat. French for "jump," sauté refers to the tossing motion used to mix the food for even cooking.

SEMOLINA FLOUR   A flour coarsely ground from durum wheat. It is used in the best pastas and in baked goods for a distinctive golden color and nutty flavor.

SERRANO CHILE   A small, thin chile pepper that is slightly tapered at the end. Ranging from dark green to scarlet in color, it is very hot, with a clean bite and a high acid level. Often substituted for the Thai chile and used frequently in salsas and sauces.

SESAME OIL   Pressed from toasted sesame seeds and used throughout Asian cuisines to add a rich, nutty flavor. Because it has a very low smoking point, it is usually added near the end of cooking.

SHIITAKE MUSHROOM A dark brown, smoky-flavored mushroom with a velvety texture. Native to Japan, it is now popular and widely cultivated in the U.S. Shiitakes are increasingly available fresh but have long been dried in China to intensify their meaty flavor. Reconstitute the dried ones in hot water for 30 minutes. Trim the woody stems of both dried and fresh mushrooms before using. Dried, they keep indefinitely in a cool, dark place; store fresh or reconstituted mushrooms in the refrigerator for 3 to 5 days.

SOY SAUCE A thin brown liquid with a pronounced saltiness that's used throughout Asia as a basic seasoning and condiment. Soy sauces vary in both thickness and sweetness.

SPRING ROLL WRAPPER A large paper-thin wrapper made from a wheat flour batter that is cooked briefly on one side, then pressed into stacks and cut into 7-inch squares. It's available refrigerated and frozen in Asian markets and larger supermarkets.

TAPIOCA STARCH A fine white starch extracted from the root of the cassava plant and used throughout Asia for thickening clear, delicately textured sauces. It is also used to strengthen doughs made of gluten-free wheat starch or rice flour.

THAI CHILE A tiny, 1-inch-long chile that is bright green, orange, or red. Also called bird's eye chiles, they are extremely hot. Substitute serranos in a ratio of 3 serrano chiles to 1 Thai chile.

TORTELLINI Small circular stuffed pastas from Italy. Said to resemble Venus's navel, they can be filled with meat or cheese, then served in a broth or drizzled with a sauce.

TORTILLA A thin, round, unleavened bread from Mexico. Made from masa or wheat flour, tortillas are cooked on a griddle, then served plain to accompany meals or used to wrap various fillings.

TORTILLA PRESS A metal utensil consisting of two flat, round surfaces and a handle that presses them together tightly to flatten dough easily and quickly into thin rounds. Used to make tortillas, the press is also perfect for forming the small, thin wrappers of Chinese steamed dumplings. Wrap the round surfaces tightly with plastic wrap to make them nonstick.

WASABI The searing yet cleansing mustard flavor of this gnarled green root, also known as Japanese horseradish, is essential as a condiment with sushi and sashimi. It is available in a powdered form (simply mix with a small amount of water) or as a paste in small jars and tubes. Store in the refrigerator indefinitely.

WATER CHESTNUT A mahogany-colored nut that grows under water. It has a thin, papery skin and sweet white flesh. Used fresh in salads or eaten as a fruit, it also retains its crisp flesh after cooking. Canned water chestnuts are widely available in supermarkets but cannot compare to the fresh ones at Asian markets. Store peeled and covered in water in the refrigerator for up to a week; change the water daily to keep fresh.

WHEAT STARCH   Wheat flour with all of its protein removed, resulting in a gluten-free, finely textured white powder. When cooked, the starch becomes completely transparent, making it an important ingredient in doughs for delicate dim sum dumplings. Available in 1-pound bags in Asian markets, it will keep indefinitely if stored tightly sealed in a cool, dark place.

WONTON WRAPPER   A Chinese noodle made of wheat, eggs, and water, rolled very thin, and cut into 3-inch squares. Wrapped around meat and vegetable fillings, wontons can be boiled for hearty soups or fried for appetizers.

ZEST   The thin, aromatic outer layer of the peel of citrus fruits. A zester conveniently removes small, curly strips. Or use a sharp paring knife to cut away only the colored part of the peel, then stack the strips and cut crosswise with a sharp knife for very thin strips. Avoid cutting into the white soft pith beneath the zest, for it is very bitter.

Index

Numbers in *italics* refer to illustrations.